CRYSTAL
Energy

Understanding and Working with Stones for Clarity and Flow

KYLE RUSSELL

Layout Design/Formatting: Susanne Clark | Creative Blueprint Design
Photographer: Raphael Brickman
Editor: Hannah Magnusson
Cover Design: Anita Lin | Mediaworks
Index: Susan Bruck

Contents

Dedication

As with all undertakings, it's wise to pay homage and establish your gratitude; offer perspective; and set your intention with vision and a mission.

Although I avoid gender in discussing particular stones, I make an exception for Mother Earth. She deserves particular consideration. Without her, we and the splendors of this planet would not exist. To her we owe the deepest thanks. We must take care of our planet ever better. We are her stewards—for better or for worse, and must humble ourselves—remembering her greatness, and that both she and the universe will outlast us.

I'd like to take this opportunity to also acknowledge and thank all the miners, known and unknown, for their efforts, toil, risk, and devotion to bringing forth treasures from the earth. They deserve our respect and admiration. I apologize for the systems in place which may not adequately compensate or protect them, and hope for better in their future.

Finally, to you, my reader. Our goal with this book is to support you in understanding crystals in new ways, enabling you to work with them more easily, and to achieve improved clarity and flow in your life.

FOUNDATION   IMAGE 1

AMAZEZ layered Amethyst cluster/root (India), more on page 108

Compassionate Oversight

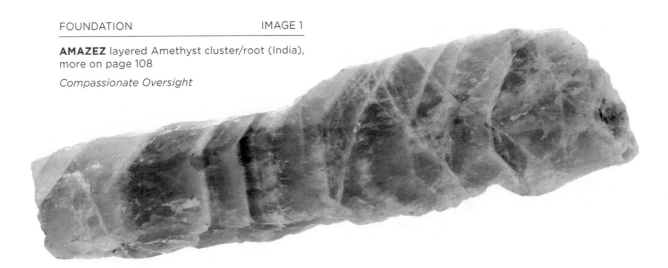

This Book is for you if...

We're all in search of a feeling—a sense of understanding, mastery, fulfillment and happiness! We want to live in a beautiful world that makes sense and feels right to us.

Exploring crystals is no different. There's so much to see and appreciate. We're all en route, but sometimes the key to this vast cache of knowledge (or that elusive experience that helps it all make sense) seems unattainable. There is so much to know and we have plenty of questions!

There are also many potential pitfalls: buying the wrong thing (including fakes), being misled by confusing or false claims and instructions, forgetting what your stones are all about (or even what they're called), and not knowing how to get to the next level in your practice of working with crystals.

What if someone could take you along the path—like a tour guide—who has already become familiar with so much of the territory?

IMAGE 2   FOUNDATION

AMMONITE fossil halved-shell (Madagascar),
more on page 108

Animal Ancestry

Having someone who knows how to hike this mountain does not take away from your own experience. In fact, it should only contribute to it. We're climbing together! What you notice and what's meaningful for you remains your own.

I've experienced breakthroughs and giant leaps in knowledge that have put me in a position to spare you years of research, trial and error. I have guided *many* people through what I call the Crystal World, and I want this book to do the same for you.

You'll benefit most from this book if any or all of these are true:

◇ **You love crystals** (you have an innate passion for stones)

◇ **You want to experience them more fully** (to share in their wonder)

- ✧ **You want to put them to use** (you feel like you could do more with them)
- ✧ **You like to learn** (you're open to new information and perspectives)
- ✧ **You're overwhelmed** (with too much confusing information out there)
- ✧ **You seek guidance** (you want to cut through the noise to find your truth)
- ✧ **You'd like a trusted source** (an approach that resonates with you)
- ✧ **You could use a logical paradigm** (to make sense of it all)

If this sounds anything like you, you're in the right place!

What's Inside

This isn't simply a quick reference guide. It's a far-reaching exploration. Now or eventually, I do recommend you read this book cover-to-cover because of the way it's been structured to address so many topics comprehensively. Look over the table of contents—jump to wherever you like, each section is super informative—but read this introduction if you'd like to have a road map. Of course, the table of contents helps too, as I've tried to provide many paths toward a common knowledge-base.

In Part One, we learn about the experiences that have brought me to share this book with you now. My earned and learned perspectives have led me to push back against—and shed new light on—the various beliefs that for many have become givens in the Crystal World and in the wider New Age community.

In Part Two, I expand on the theoretical underpinnings of how we can think about and work with stones. Exploring the applications of crystal energy will guide you further along this path, ultimately enabling you to apply the energy of crystals positively in your life.

FOUNDATION   IMAGE 3

AURALITE Amethyst root (Canada), more on page 108

Generational Layers

In Part Three, you'll see exactly how I classify the stones I find most relevant, according to my 10 Energy Zone system. There will be accompanying text and energetic descriptions, followed by an alphabetical listing, separating all the stones as either being Quartz or non-Quartz.

Please note that I use the words crystals and stones interchangeably. All crystals are stones. Not all stones are crystals.

IMAGE 4   FOUNDATION

BEDROCK (USA), more on page 109
Foundation of the Planet

Visually, the extraordinary photos of my personal collection and for-sale items drive a parallel, complementary narrative for the eye— enabling you to take in the crystals' energy directly, and if you so choose—relatively independently of the words. Each image will have its own particular explanation and is tied back to its context in the body of the book, so you can easily learn more about the significance of each one.

I do not feature any faceted gemstones, that is not my field. I find I'm better able to feel and use larger stones—including for wrapped pendants—than you're likely to have seen at a conventional jeweler or on the Home Shopping Network. My Emeralds and Herkimer Diamonds for example, although bigger, are not brilliantly colored or ultra-clear. Top grade specimens are not required, energetically, for many varieties of stones. For others, like Sugilite or Moldavite, I really prefer higher-end specimens because I feel they have that much more to offer.

As you'll witness repeatedly in this book, I'm a strong believer in both abiding by and breaking the rules. For example, most black stones are in the Channel Energy Zone, except for the ones that aren't. Polished stones are more accessible than rough stones, except when they're not. I could go on, but you'll see for yourself as you read—I'd like to think there's a method to my madness—it certainly keeps it interesting.

What I'd like you to take away and refer back to from this book as a whole is how important it is to meld the seen with the unseen, the logical with the inspirational, and the scientific with the spiritual. You should soon be armed with enough information and resources to navigate the Crystal World as well as the physical, 3D world, ever more successfully. Take my personal journey, acquired perspectives, and paradigms as pointers and as commentary. They're not the entire GPS route, just a deep exploration, to accompany your own journey.

Part 1

BACKGROUND

How I got into This

Here are some biographical tidbits from my life story that have contributed to my various philosophical perspectives.

CHILDHOOD

I grew up overseas. I was almost born in the Belgian Congo (1965) in the midst of a revolution. I still have a distinct awareness of an African elder spirit guide who watched over me there, prenatally. As it happened, my mom flew up to have me among her family in France, where I lived for my first 6 months before moving to Washington D.C.

Next we lived in Moscow (1969–72), capital of the then U.S.S.R. My parents worked for the U.S. Foreign Service, as cultural emissaries. When we came home one night to our apartment in the embassy compound, I saw a ghost in the darkened living room. I fled, bashing my head into a bookshelf, and had to get stitches in the middle of the night (without anesthetic!). It was quite an introduction to the supernatural, but I think it was an important lesson. I learned that night that ghosts can exist.

Later in Bonn, Germany (grades 2 through 5), I had recurrent dreams of a fuzzy, child-sized being that would come into my house, up to my room, whose brief finger touch would feel like scratching on a blackboard. A different dream I had several times—less jarring, fortunately—featured a silver motorcyclist riding on an endless metal rod across the desert. I saw angels coming up and down ladders a few times as well (again, all in my sleep). I had no idea what these experiences were all about at the time, but I believe they set the stage for my later, more life-changing visions.

Still in Bonn, I used to dig for small animal bones— I appreciated the odd artifact I came across, including fantastic finds at flea markets, which I relished. I acknowledged various natural places as sacred. One set of bushes near my house I called "Darti Haus" (darti was a made-up word, and haus means house or place). It was an area where unsettled spirits congregated, which I now connect to my earlier run-in with a ghost.

In the 4th grade, I remember hiking in the forests of central Europe and "remembering" my Neanderthal past. I suppose that was my first experience of a past life. I devoured books about prehistoric peoples—fascinated by evolution—and found our primordial life quite intriguing (and familiar!). I've also always been fascinated by dinosaurs, and am certain they too are part of my personal history dating back that far.

How are these stories relevant in a book about crystals? Because ultimately, becoming interested in or sensitive to the energy of crystals (I think) is connected to a larger,

IMAGE 5   FOUNDATION

COQUINA JASPER disc (India), more on page 109
Resting Place of the Ages

deeper process of opening up to the interconnectedness of transgenerational and interdimensional dynamics. As a child, my awareness had been expanded because of these waking and dreaming experiences. My hindsight is 20/20. It all makes sense now, that what I went through then, set the stage for what's happening even now.

My family visited ancient ceremonial sites in northern France (circa 1974). They resembled Stonehenge, but on a smaller scale. One was called "le tumulus," or burial mound in English, with a dark corridor we walked through. I can still hear the tour guide's impassioned tones, as he extolled its mysterious qualities. I still have a small pebble from one of the "menhirs," or tall upright stones, that had been erected there. I realize now it was that very afternoon when I first connected a piece of stone with something spiritual and timeless. I realized that rocks could be used for ceremony, ritual, and for connection with the divine. I had no idea that I would be doing this sort of thing myself, in the years to come.

Last vignette from my younger years: I was a coin and stamp collector as a kid. What I liked most about coins in particular, was that they are tangible, more three-dimensional than stamps. Crystals take that experience of dimensionality to a whole other level because they have intrinsic natural energies, which I rarely find in manufactured objects.

Being a lifelong collector is directly related to my current lifestyle and belief system. It requires careful consideration, organizing things, and thoughtful grading. That is ultimately what my 10 Energy Zone paradigm is all about. I've come up with my own method for classifying the mineral world, which works for me, and increasingly for other crystal lovers.

MIDDLE SCHOOL THROUGH COLLEGE

Moving back to the United States twice—after 5th grade and later, for college—gave me very tangible experiences as an outsider. When you live overseas, you don't belong wherever you find yourself. When you return to what's supposed to be "home," you find that you don't belong there either. It's a dynamic that gets us called "Third Culture Kids." Learning this lingo as an adult has helped me to gain perspective and to not take for granted (or put on a pedestal) any one country or way of life.

FOUNDATION   IMAGE 6

DINOSAUR GEMBONE sphere (USA), more on page 69 + 110

Prehistoric Royalty

In a different socio-economic milieu, living in Brazil for grades 9–12 (1978–1982), I saw what it was like for a country to have huge and more visible disparities in wealth than what I had seen here in the U.S., at least. Brazil has a more recent colonial past, its own population of indigenous peoples, and also a powerful African cultural influence.

I was shocked to learn that enslaving people from West Africa only stopped there in 1888, just 77 years before I was born. Percussion and dance are an important part of Brazilian culture. I attended an Afro-Brazilian Candomble religious ceremony in which the women dressed fully in white and danced for hours. The one who was possessed had nary a bead of sweat when she hugged each one of us in turn, while the drums blazed on in the background. It was mind blowing to actually witness spirit in motion.

These two elements—being myself unrooted culturally and yet being exposed to so much diversity in cultures I hadn't grown up with—made me far more open to unorthodox worldviews like the New Age consciousness I would later be exposed to, which includes the perspective that crystals might actually house inherent energies.

My family visited a mining town called Cristalina, south of Brasilia. We purchased some bookends and forgettable specimens. I had no particular affinity or interest in crystals at the time. But I guess the door was cracked open. Little did I know that I'd become a major collector of crystals in less than 10 years afterwards.

I still had to make it through school, which was not always easy. After having been behind academically for most of my life, I finished high school as valedictorian of my small class at the American School of Brasilia. I was accepted to Yale University, but didn't find it that welcoming as a campus. I was unprepared for the many schisms I encountered, by which we so readily separated ourselves from one another (and still do). There were numerous fault lines based on class, racial background, appearance, and other factors. I suppose those are commonplace everywhere, but I had come from a kinder, gentler place, so it was a rude awakening.

I was not blown away by the Ivy League experience either. Numerous classes were ho hum, but there were some bright spots. I found myself fascinated by the many obscure guest events hosted by the school. I was, however, dismayed that the majority of other students didn't care for anything beyond the mainstream. I majored in psychology and used the degree's flexibility to get credit for some memorable classes in philosophy, sociology, religion, and anthropology.

I guess this all means that by the time I was a young adult, I had seen a substantial cross section of the planet—not just geograph- ically, but geopolitically, and socially. My eyes had been opened to the good, the bad, and even the spiritual, without blinders on. I had learned to think and feel outside the box, to seek the novel and welcome the unexpected. That instinct would come in quite handy for my spiritual breakthrough, retold in this next section.

MY SPIRITUAL BREAKTHROUGH

My passionate interest in crystals took hold of me barely a year after I graduated from university. My first full time job was at a small natural food emporium called Erewhon, interestingly meant to spell nowhere backwards, as based on the 1872 book by Samuel Butler of that name. The store's long since been replaced by an antique shop at 1731 Massachusetts Avenue (Cambridge, MA), but it was the site of a most memorable supernatural encounter that changed my life forever.

IMAGE 7   FOUNDATION

ELESTIAL QUARTZ crystal (Brazil), more on page 110

Wisdom of the Ages

Let me tell you the story of what happened...

A co-worker was taking a trip to the North Shore (northeast of Boston) to visit a crystal shop on her day off, and invited me to go with her. I rearranged my schedule to make it happen and we walked in to browse the small shop "Heaven and Earth" in Gloucester. This had to have been mid-1987 (spring or early summer). The weather was nice and the day was otherwise unremarkable, but the proprietors struck me as unusual, very different somehow.

Robert Simmons and his wife Kathy were both there. As my friend milled about the tumbled stones, Robert—who's since become one of the biggest names in the Crystal World (authoring many books and building a powerful online business)—regaled me with the tale of Moldavite and how it had fallen to earth 15 million years ago. It's the only gem quality Tektite, the official name for material made up of fused extraterrestrial and earthly ingredients.

After my friend made her modest purchase and as we were leaving, Robert gifted me a small piece of Moldavite. Thinking back now, it had to be worth $50, maybe more. I was surprised but grateful, 'til we started the drive back.

I suddenly felt an enormous vortex of energy sucking the life out of me, from above and the universe, right through me and down into my pocket. It felt horribly wrong, so I took the nugget out and placed it immediately on the floor of the car.

That night when I went to bed, I placed the Moldavite up on the mantelpiece, not far from where I was sleeping. I began to dream. In the dream, I was at my food store where I was a produce clerk, arranging vegetables in the front window.

A nondescript, middle aged European looking woman—barely over 5 feet tall with short, curly blonde hair—came up to the big window pane just outside the store. She opened her mouth and let out a sound, the likes of which I'd never heard before. It was harrowing!

I've since come to recognize that sound as "harmonic singing," a wordless vocalization in which a chord is created with two or more simultaneous overtones. The Tuvan throat singers from the Himalayas do it. Back then, during the Harmonic Convergence of 1987 (the first major New Age period I was aware of, besides

FOUNDATION   IMAGE 8

PINOLITH standing slab (Switzerland), more on page 111

The Inanimate Lives!

the fabled Age of Aquarius, immortalized in the musical Hair that I was turned onto as a child), practitioners attempted harmonic signing for healing purposes through what they called "toning."

Anyhow, in the dream, I looked around to see if anyone else had heard this eerie sound. No one had. And then after a pause, and to my utter amazement, I responded using the same "language." But between what she "said" and what I replied, the intensity of the experience so rocked my world, like a nightmare, that I woke up and sat bolt upright.

I looked straight up to where I'd placed the Moldavite the night before. The connection was clear, the stone had brought about this entire interaction. I became immediately aware of what our two-phrase "conversation" had consisted of.

The lady had said, "the mothership is over us, now would be a good time to come home." I responded, "I'm not going, I refuse. I've been here too long."

Within days, I had more visions in my sleep, during which this drama played out further. I was asked by a strange (unknown, well-dressed) man to show up for a job interview somewhere, but I was instructed not to tell anyone where I was going. I took this to mean I was being set up for an abduction. Needless to say, I didn't comply.

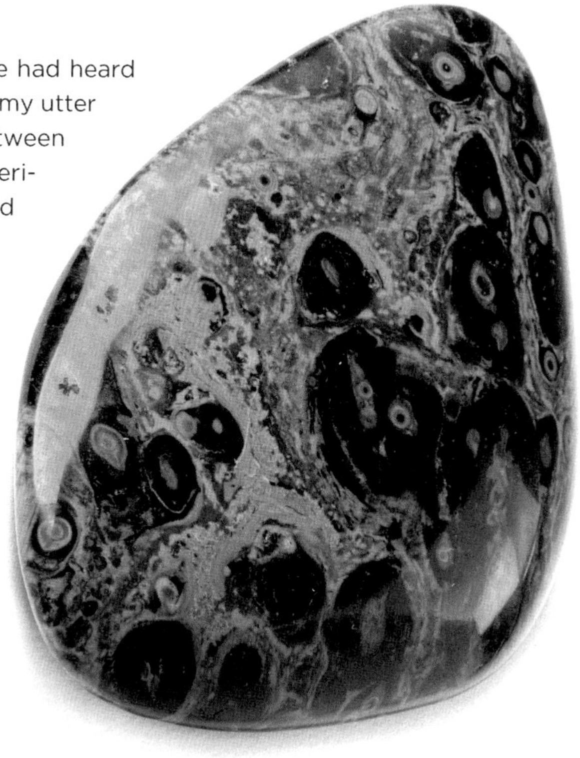

IMAGE 9   FOUNDATION

KAMBABA JASPER large freeform palm piece (Madagascar), more on page 111
Honoring All Generations of Plant Life

Then I had a dream where a different woman and I (who, while unknown, I knew was a friend) were in a great big cathedral. All the organs began to play in concert, delivering a cacophonous, deafening version of the type of expression I'd heard first from the woman outside my store window. I grabbed her hand because I knew we had to get out of the building immediately. I asserted to her—not knowing specifically what was being said by those great organs, but comprehending their import—that if we didn't get out of there quick, the entire building was doing to dematerialize with us in it.

This was all very traumatic at the time and it took 30 years for me to retell these experiences without getting goosebumps. I eschewed Moldavite for 20 of those years because it felt anathema to my existence here on earth. As someone who'd chosen a terrestrial life, it felt unnatural to connect with something so otherworldly.

I'd had cancer twice, when I was 12 and 18, so I knew what it felt like to be pushed up against the veil, near death and expulsion from this mortal coil. It took some doing, but I had decided—and acted accordingly—not to cross over to the other side, and to instead stay here.

Even after this supernatural occurrence—when I was almost killed in a robbery and when one of my children was almost carried away by a rushing river, all worst-case scenarios—I managed to hold onto life with a steady stream of good luck and perseverance.

My commitment to the living and my continuing desire to dwell on this planet contributes to the fulfillment I get from sharing my experiences and understanding for the betterment of others. My ultimate goal is for you to comprehend—to the best of my ability to express it, and yours to assimilate it—what a powerful role stones can play in our lives.

But how is my passion for stones connected to my close encounter with the aliens? Besides the fact that it was brought on by a Moldavite, something equally surprising happened as a result. Within two weeks of my various transformative waking and sleeping experiences, I discovered that I suddenly knew all kinds of things about crystals!

ROOT   IMAGE 10

DRAGON QUARTZ cluster, iron colored (Morocco), more on page 60 + 112
Life Fire, Doing and Being Energy

I had miraculously become what I call geo-sentient. By that, I mean I had become sensitive to the energies of stones in a very specific way. I suddenly knew intuitively how to feel and focus crystal energies.

I have no doubt in my mind (or heart) that this new wealth of knowledge and understanding was 100% because of the Moldavite and the proximity and visitations by the extraterrestrials.

A breakthrough had happened. I had gone from considering rocks inanimate and irrelevant to a deep knowledge that they can be quite impactful. They are rife with positive energies, capable of imparting benefits to our lives that are far beyond our expectations, or even comprehension.

It's amazing how seemingly chance encounters can have such broad-ranging implications.

That's it for my earlier life biographical preamble. It sets the chronological timeline for my spiritual development, and explains the circumstances that made me who I am today, a bona fide crystal guide.

SELF-TRANSFORMATION FROM HEALER TO EDUCATOR

For the first 25 years I was into crystals, I used them for individual healing work, which began immediately and professionally in 1987. I was suddenly able to recognize people's past lives. I've since lost that ability, but I don't mourn it for the same reason I've not been taken by the study or observance of astrology. While I'm the last to deny the power of distant times and places, I also believe we have more than enough information right here and from this lifetime to focus on, as we grapple with our innumerable current issues.

It was certainly exciting to help people get rid of spirits trapped unhappily on this side. I was approached to do black magic hex work, but I always refused. After those first few years, only friends and family benefited from my various talents while I pursued other professional goals. I had two shops selling international clothing and jewelry, created and published a world music magazine, and pursued a recording and performance career as a bassist and band leader. Oh, and I got married and had two lovely children, now 18 and 21 years old. All that kept me quite busy!

By 2012 though, I was back in the Crystal World, compelled to teach my first class. I had to begin systematizing my knowledge, getting it out of my head. I had attended and presented at some new age expos along the way, but I realized that my new goal was to teach people how to understand and work with crystals themselves.

At first, my lessons were clunky (in retrospect) but informative. One concept I came up with was to suggest people consider what I called my various "axes of analysis." When looking at a crystal, ask yourself if it is light or heavy, plentiful or rare, rough or polished? Is it cheap or expensive, a power stone or "just a rock?" It was an interesting exercise—still probably useful—but ultimately, it didn't survive as a particular tool I still use for teaching.

What remains is the hallmark of my work with people and crystals. It's what I call The Inquiry. Later, in Part Two, you'll see more about how it's applied with individuals. For the stones themselves, it's

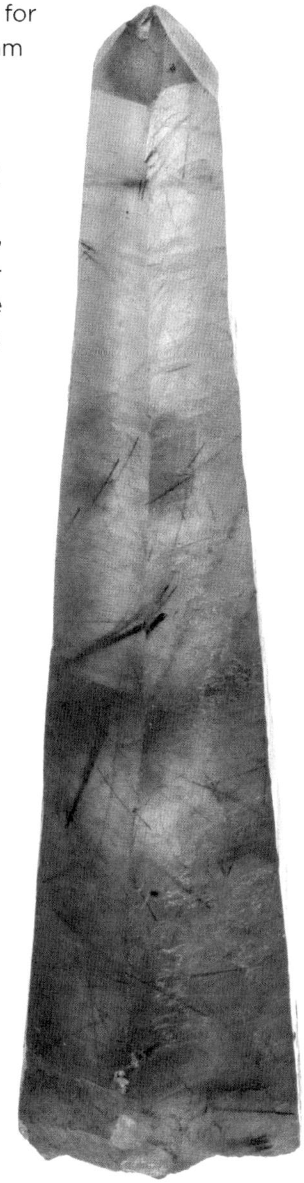

IMAGE 11   ROOT

EDENITE laser wand point (Madagascar), more on page 112

Power of Growing Plants and Seasons

about collecting information to identify their unique energy signatures. What I pick up on about a stone is not random or exclusively intangible. I take into consideration their visual complexity (like the patterns on Charoite and Seraphinite for example), the different sensations produced, their look and feel, and their relative density.

Repetition and fine tuning over the years have done wonders in helping me articulate what was something of a diamond in the rough. I had all kinds of internal knowledge that needed polishing for better presentation. Doing that has enabled me to give you the answers I now have, so you're not re-inventing the wheel in terms of determining which stones symbolize what. It's also what allows me to continue my explorations and learn about the energies of stones I haven't really spent time with yet, or have not yet fully understood.

For the next 8 years, I hosted many workshops and meditations. I've even hosted a few retreats. Themes ranged from "The Wonders of Quartz" to exploring particular chakras. A popular offering I had was called "The Crystal Heart." Soon I was putting out videos on YouTube and leading webinars, all of which has prepared me for this increasingly virtual age of online learning.

ROOT   IMAGE 12

HEMATITE geometric formation (Brazil), more on page 113

Grounding Connectedness

What Makes Me Different

As someone who's totally sold on the metaphysical relevance of crystals, I am still a critical thinker. I don't accept everything I read or hear, without questioning. As I recommend you do as well, I use my own good judgement, based on my own considerable experience and wisdom.

Decades of exposure to New Age thinking and Crystal Lore have shown me a number of beliefs that I simply don't adhere to. Not that they're all bad or baseless, but I'm not coming from a place of accepting them at face value, without scrutiny. Examining them with me here not only helps you to identify what makes my approach unique, but it also might help you think through these ideas when you come across them yourself.

Engaging New Age Paradigms

1. I BELIEVE IN **WALKING THE WALK**

The idea of walking the walk, or putting your money where your mouth is, was not invented by New Age thinkers. But it's definitely expected among New Age adherents, or light workers as they often consider themselves, that you live by the lofty tenets which you espouse. As in any community, those who actually live by its highest standards are often in the minority.

I can't speak for anybody else, but I'm proud that I've made some real concessions to my beliefs, modifying my lifestyle in specific ways that have governed my choices for years. Granted, I did so out of a sense of self preservation. So I don't expect a medal for it.

Let me explain a bit further. I hadn't mentioned this earlier, but I had a hard childhood in my family of origin. It was a volatile environment. Although I experienced wonderful places growing up, I believe that getting cancer twice was my body's response to a toxic environ-ment, first at home and then at university, and in reaction to what I experienced as the stultifying impact of mainstream culture.

To get my life back, I had to make two major changes. First I became vegan for seven years as a body cleanse, and then I had to let go of others' expectations of me, pursuing my own interests in order to not self-destruct.

What this has meant, practically, is that I've entered into a con-scious relationship with my lifestyle. Sugar, for example, took me 30 years to fully wean myself off of. Breaking out of the corporate and generally accepted professional employment model—and being self-employed for over 30 years has not been easy—but it's been the right thing to do (for me).

There have been failures and setbacks, which I've bounced back from, just as I did against cancer all those years ago. New Age literature and coaches often urge us to do what we love and everything will fall into place. It sounds almost self indulgent. They brag about how it's

IMAGE 13 ——————————————————— ROOT

IRON METEORITE, Campo Del Cielo (Argentina),
more on page 114

Grounding, from Space to the Core

worked for them, but I think we all have our own way to go. There's no one-size-fits-all solution to our problems, or any guaranteed pot of gold just over the horizon.

What I'm saying here is: don't believe the hype. Do what you're doing not because of some promised (automatic) reward you're supposed to get, but because the journey *itself* is the reward. You should follow your life's path, struggles and all. Be compelled to fulfill your own destiny, however that's been revealed to you.

For me, that's meant living by, and pursuing my knowledge of crystals. It's given me the great gift of being able to teach about them, interact with them, and buy and sell them. This is my life's work and I'm fully engaged with it.

2. I BELIEVE THAT **INSPIRATION SHOULD MEET LOGIC**

I find that the matte finish of practicality is the ultimate balance for the glitter of the stars. Hence my belief in the importance of logic and common sense, which are often under-championed among New Age perspectives.

In an ideal New Age world, wishing for things would be enough to bring them into being. There's a dynamic called spiritual bypassing that involves sweeping complex issues under the spiritual carpet. I don't believe that a conviction that we're facing a new dawn of world peace is enough to make that actually happen.

I know it's a tough trade-off, but I prefer to think of it more like a dance. You definitely need dreams to start somewhere, so that you can envision the future you want to make happen. It's important to have ideas, fantasies, and hopes. I was inspired in this way to go ahead with writing this book. But without hard work, resources, a team, and a strong sense of management, none of it would have been possible.

ROOT   IMAGE 14

RED JASPER large chunk (Brazil), more on page 114

Balanced Life Force

So yes, leaps of faith are necessary. I cannot explain or provide a rational underpinning for all my beliefs. That's how they were ushered in, mysteriously. I continue to have to tap into that creative source. But in this book and in general, I will do my best to "show my work" so that you can follow along and make as much sense of what I'm sharing as possible.

3. I BELIEVE THAT
NO, IT'S NOT YOUR FAULT

There's a New Age worldview by which it becomes your fault that you're ill, and it's your fault if you can't navigate your way completely back to health.

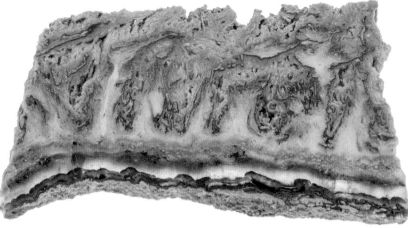

IMAGE 15   ROOT

SATIN FLASH OPAL slab (USA), more on page 115

Blazing through the Ages

Yes, there are steps you could've taken to not get ill, but you've seen the stories about 90-year-old smokers, fit as a fiddle with hardly a weakness. You also hear stories about young people taken for no apparent reason, with zero pre-existing conditions or issues on their health record.

We don't have as much control over reality as many New Agers would have us believe. We can't simply pass go and collect $200. Law of Attraction. Prosperity consciousness. These are some of the Ten Commandments of New Age theology. But anyone who's self-employed knows it's never that easy.

Things fluctuate. My take home lesson from my first experiences in retail? It doesn't always get better.

One thing I can share from my career in music (and you can see it from most artists' life stories) is that inevitably you peak, then decline. Nothing lasts forever. Spirit is not always with you, putting wind in your sails. Although we can all aspire to emulate the best sailors, who learn nimbly how to adapt to the changing winds, for many of us that can be a fleeting dream.

There's something called survivorship selection bias. It's easy if the world has smiled upon you to cast aspersions on those who haven't made it. You can't simply will a seven-figure income into being. Many still argue that you can, and that if you don't, you should only blame yourself. They'll say, "You're simply not trying hard (or smart) enough. You just don't have the right mindset."

It's a double-edged sword, this New Age mentality. There's also something very American: "Lift yourself up by your bootstraps!" about it. It has its merits, it can be empowering—but on the flip side—it can also be quite deflating and harmful (blaming the victim), in its own unique way.

I come from a different place, where I see that shaming judgment is not really helpful and a high degree of authentic self-compassion is actually required. I'm not recommending that you be spiritually lazy—or justify actual wrongdoing—but merely that you do what you can and leave the rest to G8D (my spelling, in an effort not to use the creator's name in vain, but also to add a sense of infinity to it, with the number 8).

We only have so much control over our destiny. Luck is a real thing. That's a wind source in itself and, like a sailor, you have to navigate and swing your sails around just so, to catch or ride it whenever it comes and wherever it takes you.

4. I BELIEVE IN **THE SPIRIT OF CREATION**

I don't let religion, following the letter of the law, get in the way of spiritualism—which is the actual spirit of supreme, universal, or natural law. Put differently, I believe most in the law of spirit. It's bigger than any one religion. While most religions and New Age philosophies are categorical and exclusive in their claim to have a lock on truth, I accept that there can be multiple, co-existing truths. There is not always one correct answer.

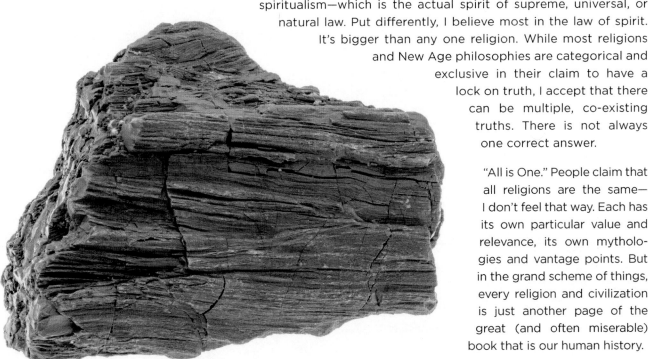

"All is One." People claim that all religions are the same— I don't feel that way. Each has its own particular value and relevance, its own mythologies and vantage points. But in the grand scheme of things, every religion and civilization is just another page of the great (and often miserable) book that is our human history.

ROOT   IMAGE 16

RED PETRIFIED WOOD log (USA),
more on page 115

Igniting the Fire Below

Stand up for what you believe in now and adhere to what you accept as your own true path, but know and recognize the impermanence of everything, including your own ideology, thoughts, and existence. I realize this sounds a bit nihilistic, I suppose I'm an existentialist in this way.

At the end of the day, all we have is our precious, fleeting lives, our values and our commitments.

Whatever your beliefs, I certainly hope you'll agree that a credence in crystals does not (and should not) threaten any of them. Crystals are part of G8D's creation (just like scripture) and to use and appreciate them is a celebration of the creator, however you conceive of her, him, or it.

But is it idol worship to imbue inanimate objects like stones and crystals with extraordinary powers? Does recognizing and harnessing crystals' inherent energies bypass, or disrespect our honor for the creator? I think neither. Belief in the power of crystals is a broadened appreciation of the encompassing power of the divine. They are unique tools among many that G8D has given us to manifest holy will, if we so choose to use them in that way.

IMAGE 17   ROOT

RED CAP AMETHYST aka Super Seven Type 2 twin points (Brazil) more on page 116 + 136

Emerging from Source

If you are agnostic or atheistic, this perspective should likewise make sense. I think anytime somebody's fearful or judgemental of others' beliefs—particularly when they do not actually impact them in any way—it's time to really look in the mirror and assess how true to spirit you're really being.

5. I BELIEVE IN **THE DANCE OF THE METAPHYSICAL WITH THE PHYSICAL WORLD**

I do think there is at least one parallel universe, maybe more, in addition to our day-to-day, tactile experience. The first peoples of Australia call it the Dreamtime. I will use this word freely, but I am not schooled in the subtleties of their use of it. For me, this Dreamtime coincides and sometimes collides with what we generally or collectively call reality.

It's a dance, for sure, between these worlds. What happens here can affect what happens there, and vice versa. This complex interrelationship is not surprising to the New Age mind.

What makes my perspective different is that I don't idealize it. I admit: the dance has its missteps, as anyone who has experienced tears of sorrow or unexpected (and unwanted) tears in The Matrix, can attest to.

The Matrix, made famous by the movie of that name, is an interesting construct. Again, I'm employing it for my own purposes, so your best definition in the context of this book comes from how I apply it here.

My concept of the matrix is similar to the matrix or rough material from which crystals emerge. The hard shell around an Amethyst geode or the Dolomitic Sandstone that births Herkimer Diamonds is considered its matrix material. The matrix is basically the womb from which the primordial ooze produces and sustains new life, whether organic or inorganic.

Our personal matrix is the gestalt or entirety of everything surrounding us—our friends and family, upbringing, education, job, neighborhood, etc. When things are going well, all is good in our matrix. An accident, divorce, natural disaster, these can all cause or reflect tears in the matrix. I would argue that these sorts of occurrences are at least in part due to upheaval or discord on this and/or the other side of the veil.

Animist and shamanic beliefs take this all in stride. And while I'm no expert in either field, I think they'd agree with me that the other side is not all peace and love. It has the same (and some separate) challenges and conflicts going on, just like what we grapple with on this more mundane plane.

ROOT   IMAGE 18

RED LASER QUARTZ wand point (Madagascar), more on page 116

Focused Life Energy

I've found many New Agers who prefer to believe that everything is beautiful on the other side. They embrace it like it's their concept of heaven. Some people and belief systems reserve ambivalence and turmoil exclusively for purgatory and hell. If only it were that simple.

Most people live their entire lives trapped in the physical three-dimensional, but if you can navigate and take heed of the signs and signals from the other side, you will be living in greater harmony with the larger universe. Becoming sensitive to alternate planes means that your sails are getting sensitive to the winds that arise from multiple dimensions. This provides new and different ways to navigate more expertly, with a fuller sense and experience of multi-dimensional reality.

I believe that heaven, hell, and purgatory are all here too—and that we can experience different proportions of each on either side.

If this "other side" is so important, and its impact is so real, why can't we prove its existence scientifically? We can't. If it were of this world, we could. The very fact of its being of and from another dimension makes it untouchable, unquantifiable, and unmeasurable in conventional terms.

Actually, when I say it's untouchable, I mean mostly to the hand or scientific instruments. In fact, it's very touchable in other ways. That's what psychics and mediums specialize in. They reach over and back between the worlds with ease.

My main approach to working with these other planes of existence is—not surprisingly—to use crystals to project and receive information from (or to) "over there." And over there is not just outside of us. This Dreamtime is very much embedded within us too, in our mind, body, and subconscious.

The language of the Dreamtime is sensation, visioning, signs and wonders. Life circumstances, misfortunes, hopes, and dreams are all ways that we can hear loud and clear what's going on just across the veil. Our capacity to listen, navigate, adapt, and strive are all ways we talk back to and enter into dialog with, The Matrix.

IMAGE 19   ROOT

RHODOCHROSITE botryoidal formation (Argentina), more on page 116

Physical Renewal

6. I BELIEVE THAT **EVIL IS A THING**

In the natural world, predators don't hate their prey. Call hatred an outgrowth of civilization, maybe connect it to the pecking order of herds and wolves, putting its origins right back within Nature. Exploitation, jealousy, domination, revenge, these are all aspects of evil, regardless of their origin, and they are meant to intentionally harm or subjugate others.

I was surprised to hear some witches say there's no such thing as black magic. There has to be. Why wouldn't people, so able to use every other sphere of human endeavor to try to manipulate others and produce more favorable outcomes for themselves, not employ metaphysical methods to do the same?

When I was in Peru, where it's generally stated that there's no more human sacrifice, one of our tour guides (who was the only one allowed to take us into a particular area) suggested otherwise. In my worldview, it's hard to construe human sacrifice or cannibalism as justifiable. But our social constructs are not universal and certainly haven't been, historically. Remember that not so long ago, slavery was legal and that it and its legacy lives on today.

Regardless of perspective or historical relativism, it's easy to find examples through history of bold-faced evil, perpetrated mostly by men against others. The toxic masculine contiues to take its toll. As a race, we have real trouble learning from our mistakes. So we are condemned to repeat them until we can finally learn the lesson and primacy of love.

We don't need karma, reincarnation, or religious texts to prove all this. We have only to look at the present and not so distant past to see evils—including racism, hypocrisy, greed and pollution—all reproducing themselves like a virus, propagating easily throughout the population.

How does this relate to crystals? I believe evil can be lodged in certain (very few) crystals because of wicked human intention. Certain types of crystals can be "un-lifeful" too, but naturally, meaning they can harm us automatically. Radioactive material obviously fits into this category.

I also believe that crystals can be used to reverse some of these effects. Given enough time, a Smoky Quartz has transmuted even something as toxic as radioactivity. Ultimately, most human harm can be undone through human good will.

As Martin Luther King said, "Hate cannot drive out hate, only love can do that."

ROOT   IMAGE 20

RHODONITE palm piece (Brazil), more on page 117

Supporting Possibility

7. I BELIEVE IN THE **WONDERS OF MEDICINE**

If you've been a New Ager for long, you've known or heard of people who've rejected medical treatment. They're convinced that they can heal themselves. That happens, but mostly anecdotally. The fact is that it doesn't produce reliable outcomes. We all want that power and control, but it takes a lot of self-discipline and the gift of good fortune to overcome an illness all on your own. And the results are not guaranteed.

Let me paraphrase from the familiar parable of a man recently passed, shaking his fist at G8D as he stands at the pearly gates. "I drowned, waiting for you to save me, why didn't your outstretched hand lift me up from the waves (as I had expected it would)?" And the Creator replies, "I sent you a rope, a life saver, and the coast guard, but you rejected all that help, waiting for me to save you according to some fantasy you concocted in your mind, instead of the reality of what resources I had made clearly and presently available to you."

Science and Medicine are gifts we are blessed to benefit from in this day and age. We must take advantage of them to the fullest. I know I made it through my cancers because of medical interventions and I'm grateful for them.

But the flipside—an unquestioning faith in Medicine—is also not helpful. The hospitals have not figured it all out. Remember that it's called the *practice* of medicine. Doctors are still working out the kinks and learning so much through research, trial, and error each year.

I've often heard that hospitals are the worst places to be if you're not feeling well. Malpractice aside, the energy of so many sick people, the lack of warmth, the sterility—these are not so hospitable. Lapses in service happen often enough and the barely edible food hardly makes it a nourishing place to convalesce.

Beyond the issues in hospitals, there are still incurable viruses afoot and illnesses that are fully capable of taking their toll regardless of treatments. How many suffer from undiagnosed or unidentified maladies? Auto-immune diseases like Lyme are perfect examples of conditions for which there are only imperfect treatment plans.

The medical establishment treats us like cars, machines. It determines, in the greatest number of cases, what is most likely to fix our engines. But remember the disclaimers you sign before going under the knife. Doctors protect themselves from contingencies because they know they are not omnipotent and things don't always go according to plan.

Our job as energy workers picks up where the doctors' leave off. We fill in the blanks, take on the matters of spirit that they are both unqualified and uninterested in pursuing.

"We do not live by bread alone." That old saying captures it well. We are so much more than the sum of our organs and vessels. Our life energy is not like the ignition of a car, it can't be turned on and off automatically. We operate according to rules and relationships that far exceed what's visible to the naked eye or the microscope.

The worlds and dynamics beyond the grasp of technicians are the worlds that crystals can help us navigate, which gives them a unique advantage in those realms.

IMAGE 21   ROOT

RUBY crystal (India), more on page 118
Stone Grounding, Point Zero

8. I BELIEVE THAT **SCIENCE IS OUR FRIEND**

I've been called to task by folks who brand crystal healing as quackery. They attribute any benefits derived solely to the placebo effect. Mostly, they take issue with the fact that crystal energies and their positive effects cannot be measured by any known instruments.

We've established earlier that the metaphysical world is necessarily immune to hard measurement. I beg to differ. We actually have a perfectly good instrument capable of measuring and experiencing crystal energies and those of the "other side" alike. Hello?! If the human mind and body can feel it—and we are such a complex creation that nobody's been able to replicate *us*—then rest assured, we *do* have an instrument right here that is quite capable of measuring these energies: our very own selves!

Well then why, they might ask, can't what happens for you be replicated in the lab through controlled experiments? Because what's happening when we work metaphysically is not a universally measurable physical process or reaction. You cannot track it the way you do with the effect of drugs or other medical interventions on the generally similar human body.

I've learned time and again that despite commonalities, most people will experience an individual or type of crystal completely differently from their neighbor.

I have no quarrel with science. I have the utmost respect for the experts. I don't side with those who question climate change or the cause, symptoms, and precautions we need to take around pandemics like COVID, which has scourged us so thoroughly as I write this. Places where the far right and the far left concur—siding against science, the experts, vaccinations, and instead embracing conspiracy theories—that's not where I'm at.

Not that I don't have a healthy skepticism of "the system." It and the powers that be, even the mainstream media, have their fair share of flaws and bad actors. I actually think mainstream culture is more hazardous than its media. But to reflexively throw out the baby with the bathwater, in favor

ROOT   IMAGE 22

TIGER IRON, standing polished freeform (Madagascar), more on page 118

Blended Roots

of even less qualified so-called whistleblowers or false prophets with their own shadowy intentions, does not strike me as the wisest alternative.

Whether in medicine, science, or even politics, I believe we should work with what we have to get to a better place. Tearing it all down could take us back to the Middle Ages, or worse. The important advances of recent centuries—in every sphere of life—should be built upon. Dismantle or remodel as necessary, but don't simply destroy them because they're flawed. Anarchy is not what we want or need.

This is in stark contrast to what I've heard in New Age circles, that a golden age of transformation is right around the corner, or already upon us, and that without any an effort, things will magnificently transform and we will enjoy a new dawn of peace and brotherly/sisterly love together. It's a form of messianism, where the intercession of some divine being will make everything okay. And we'll all be saved from the fate we so richly deserve.

IMAGE 23   BELLY

CARNELIAN palm piece (Madagascar),
more on page 119

Deep Body Functions

My view of human-kind is far more cynical than that. Yes, we should wave the banner of harmony, but nothing I've seen in terms of the advances we treasure (socially or technologically) comes easily, without hard work or sacrifice.

Ultimately, we need to figure out the whole cooperation and coexistence thing far better than we have thus far. Making use of all spheres of human expertise is imperative to our long term success.

To close out this section, I want to be clear that I absolutely consider myself to have way more in common with New Agers than most others. We appreciate the spiritual, we're trying to make the world a better place. And we're willing to look within.

I don't want my efforts to distinguish myself to be construed as not endorsing most New Age beliefs. I just want to be able to live them more authentically, with an eye toward practicality, and in a way that's not disrespectful of people's varying capacity to effect change in their lives. I'm willing to embrace the metaphysical with no illusions about its perfection or limitations. When it comes to science and medicine, all are welcome at the table. The end goal is to help you as the individual, by whatever means necessary.

Rethinking Crystal Myths

To begin with, we have to ask ourselves, "What is a myth?" Myths are stories created or passed along traditionally, which explain customs, history, or natural phenomena.

A perfect example of this would be the creation myth, which varies from culture to culture. And now we have scientific theory, which contradicts them all. Unless you believe as I do: that fact and fiction can peacefully (and productively) coexist, as do the physical and metaphysical planes.

Most educated people believe, in our culture, that traditional Myths are simply bunk—made up falsehoods that are used to explain what happened before, with moral implications for what goes on today. They read them at services and hear sermons about them as a quaint formality. I think they have allegorical worth. For instance, the story of Adam and Eve teaches us about choice and the mixed blessing of having eaten from the tree of knowledge.

Conversely, we can be lulled into a false reassurance by myth. Take for example the American Dream, it's not equally available to everyone. Liberty and justice are regrettably not for all in the United States, much as we might want to pretend that they are.

Similarly, in the crystal lore that has built up over the past number of decades, there are beliefs that many take for granted as a given. I don't accept many of them because my source of information was so direct, personal, and distinctive. I pick up the books and look online, but before long I have to look away.

Read on to see why. Don't take my word for it. See what resonates and let go of the rest. Just know that I've thought about these divergences of vision for some time, and I've consistently arrived at the same conclusions you'll see outlined below.

BELLY IMAGE 24

FAUX CITRINE aka Baked Amethyst
cluster (Brazil), more on page 119

Useful Transformation

1. CLEANSING AND CLEARING (ARE NOT ALWAYS REQUIRED)

To suggest the notion of not cleansing or clearing is heresy, given the ubiquitous commands throughout the Crystal World to do both. Roughly speaking, cleansing removes external gunk and clearing removes internal gunk.

People think, "Oh, all those people (and their energy) who've touched this stone, I need to liberate it from their karma." Fair enough, I'll never say never, but I strongly believe stones come with their own protections or internal integrity, and are not as susceptible to being corrupted as folks imagine.

If a crystal is physically dirty, soap and water is good enough. Avoid salt, it's corrosive! Goo Gone is great for sticker adhesive. Be careful though, with Amber. When polished, its surface can dull and be damaged with even the utmost TLC. These are all surface treatments, as the goal is to not mess with what's inside, energetically.

If the crystal's been around severely confused or ill-intentioned people, I can also understand the need to give it a fresh start, using the commonly accepted techniques of sage burning, sound healing, sun and moonlight, even burying it in the ground. None of these methods hurt on the face of it, again because they're external and respectful of the crystal's inherent vibration or energy signature.

IMAGE 25 BELLY

GREEN OPAL, palm piece (Madagascar), more on page 120

Honoring Your Internal Organs

Where we get into trouble, is when we clear reflexively and unnecessarily. I learned this the hard way. One of the first crystals I ever got was a wonderful Emerald cluster. It packed quite a punch, with a buzz I really appreciated (though I never truly understood what it was about until relatively recently). I cleansed/cleared it—as I'd been told to, since I was new to this and didn't know any better. Instead of just giving it a topical cleanse though, I somehow wiped the entire hard drive. It lost everything it had. Nothing was left. Even now, all these years later, I cannot re-access that glory it once shared so freely.

Crystals are like trees. You can see phantoms in some crystals—a little ghost image of an earlier stage of that crystal, when it was smaller—because it has some sort of residue on that earlier incarnation of itself that makes it stand out from the rest of the clear crystal (that grew before, around and above it, afterwards). Don't worry, I have a photo of a phantom here in this book, to make it easier to grasp what I'm talking about. It's nice to consider those rings or layers to be symbolic of years and changes gone through, like wisdom, acquired over time.

Whether you can see those growth rings or not (it's not just a physically visible phenomenon) it's metaphorical (and actual) on different levels. Any stone has been through a lot—thousands, even millions of years of its own history. As such, it has to have absorbed some large measure of knowledge and wisdom over that time period, simply as a result of its longevity and exposure to earth elements above and below ground. We want to honor, preserve, and protect the message each crystal has for us. We don't want to remove its whole history and breadth of knowledge, making it an empty shell of its former self.

To return to the computer metaphor, say you get a fully featured, brand new computer loaded with software. It's plug and play. Do you start by erasing the hard drive and starting all over again? No. That makes zero sense, given how useful all that software is.

BELLY   IMAGE 26

MANGO QUARTZ tumbled point (Madagascar), more on page 120
Nourshing Passage

If you truly believe you've inherited a defective product, one with a virus in it, you may think you'd like to save it, like a good Samaritan. Interesting what a human instinct this is. Folks who proselytize, religiously or otherwise, are also motivated to save your soul in this same way. They have a burning desire to change you from what you are to what they'd *rather* you be. This is exactly the wrong approach. It's very anti-Nature and flows from the concept of original sin—that things (and people) start out flawed and need to be corrected, or "brought into the light."

The way things are going and the way they end up cyclically in our society, I can relate to the need for us to be saved from our own self-destructive tendencies. Yes we may need help, but I don't believe that we are intrinsically broken inside. We just need to acknowledge and build on our better instincts.

Think of the incalculable damage the idea that we are "bad" has done psychologically to humans over the millennia. For her part, I don't believe Mother Nature has made crystals defective in any way. They would not have made it this far if they could not hold their own. And you wouldn't be attracted to them if not for the intrinsic qualities and strengths they show you when you first meet.

If you get a lemon—something that really doesn't agree with you—return it, pass it along. One person's trash is another's treasure. It might resonate differently, or better, in someone else's hands.

Unfortunately, in a rare number of cases, it's possible for stones to have been imbued with evil, through human intention. Dealing with hexes and negative witchcraft, you can learn more about in the Crystals for Life section. In those cases, "don't try this at home." Exorcism or confronting demons is not to be taken on lightly, or by novices.

What if a stone has been influenced by some other, non-human force supernaturally? Take even the piece of Moldavite that catapulted me so forcefully into the Crystal World. What it brought was totally alien, so intense and challenging to my existence that I had to get rid of it. Note that I didn't try to "cure" it or use "conversion therapy" to make it be what it was not. I simply passed it along to someone who appreciated it more, even though it was not as transformative for them as it was for me.

Why not just experience stones for what they are, rather than projecting or trying to re-create some idealized pure-state that we as newcomers (infants in the grand scheme of geological time) believe we can restore them to?

2. **DON'T PROGRAM** (*THEY* AREN'T THE ONES THAT NEED HELP)

I spoke extensively above, regarding clearing and cleansing. Let me explain how programming is different. To cleanse is like taking a shower, to clear is like detoxing. To program, on the other hand, is essentially to brainwash.

The intention may be good—and for positive purposes—but the ends do not justify the means.

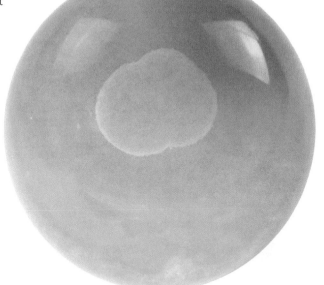

Let me push the point a bit further, hopefully without overstating it. Programming crystals (or another fancy word for this is "entrainment") is like mansplaining or imperialism. At its worst, it's ultimately about domination and exploitation. Bending the will of the stone to do your bidding is attempting to entrap and control it. I oppose this approach out of respect for the stones. If you really want to honor your crystals, don't program them.

It is *we* who need the programming. *We're* the ones with the baggage, trying to change *our* world. They've already perfected what they came here to be. The stones come to us with a pure vibration that we may borrow, make use of, or focus for our own purposes, but our intention should never be to overwrite their innate and pre-existing programming.

There is a level of dignity that the stones possess. Our job should be to allow for that always, not to consider every stone an empty vessel that's waited thousands of years for us to rescue them and replace their innate qualities with our own human intentions.

IMAGE 27 BELLY

ORANGE CALCITE sphere (Mexico),
more on page 69 + 120

Soothing Flow

3. GRIDS DON'T FIX (ON THEIR OWN)

A lot of folks put a huge amount of stock in crystal grids. Basically, they're like a board game. You're instructed to fill it in with certain particular stones to effect some sort of shift of the matrix in your favor.

That's not a bad idea, and if it makes you feel like you're getting a handle on something in your life, more power to you (and it). I get that making this seem easy is a worthy goal, particularly for beginners. My concern is that it feels contrived and ingenuine.

Using those same stones in a simpler configuration or in, as I call it, a constellation can do the same thing without it feeling like a set-it-and-forget-it confabulation.

What is a constellation? It's a few, thoughtfully selected stones that are organized synergistically with a single or set of intentions in mind. It's not the layout that matters, per se. The grid is not doing the work. Remember, it's the stones themselves doing the work. All you're doing is pairing their elemental energies toward some higher purpose.

Say, for example, you're wanting to tackle some health problem. Later (in the Crystals for Life section), I do discuss some particularly recommended stones I have for this. But in broad strokes, you might want to pick one for grounding, one for vitality, and one for realignment to keep it simple. I like doing basic triangles, circles, and cross formations. Sometimes I surround them in a circle with spacers or equilibrium stones (for example bean pods or Apache Tear Obsidian) to create a more sacred space. Together they mirror your hopes and they multitask energetically, with an eye toward bettering your situation.

My preference is for people to think more and deeply about what they're doing. I've often said, "this is a participatory, not a spectator sport." To get the most out of it, it's actually better if you don't paint by the numbers.

You might ask, "Isn't something better than nothing?" Sure. It's like exercise—two minutes may not be equal to 20 minutes of exertion, but it's always better than nothing.

Use your grids if you must, especially for training. But ultimately, for what I think are the best results, you should step out on a limb and

BELLY · IMAGE 28

TANGERINE QUARTZ relationship stones (Brazil), more on page 121

Calm Coating

find your own way. It's like swimming or riding a bike. Folks can only hold your hand for so long before you charge out into the horizon on your own steam.

4. CRYSTALS ARE NOT OUR SERVANTS

Many people ask, "What does this crystal do? What is it good for?" While it's true that each has its own energy field, which can impact its surroundings in a specific way, the stones don't exist to do our bidding. They do what they do, they are what they are, regardless of us. They've been here for millennia before us and they'll survive us as well. To think otherwise is simply human ego.

Yes, make use of them, appreciate and connect with them, but give them the respect they are due. It's like the custom of many Indigenous peoples that teaches us to step lightly on the earth, so that it might continue to provide for future generations. That is an inspiring example of how to think about and interact with the elements.

IMAGE 29   SELF

AMETRINE leaning cathedral generator/ transmitter (Bolivia), more on page 59 + 122

Balancing Self with Mission

What irks me most in the crystal lore is the presumptuousness or entitlement required to think that we can affect the universe with only the most passive input on our part. It's like you want to set up an instant interface with the Universal—make it as easy as getting an internet connection—and that armed with the magic password, the matrix will automatically open up and share with you its bounties.

I wish it were that easy, or do I? I like the idea of tapping into Spirit just like that, and working it smoothly for positive effect. But in reality, it's work, it's effort, it's engagement. It's a solemn commitment, not to be taken on frivolously.

5. CRYSTALS DON'T CHANGE (MOST OF THE TIME)

I've encountered numerous folks who've claimed that their crystals have transformed over time, becoming cloudy, darker, lighter—even shape shifting to look different than they once did. I have never had this experience, which might speak somehow to my relationship with crystals, and I wonder about these other people. Is there something awry in their relationship with their crystals? I don't know.

Certainly, too much sunlight can bleach out color, particularly in Amethyst. But getting darker? I can only imagine this is because the crystal is taking on some kind of gunk. It's believable, it just hasn't happened to me.

Of course, there are mechanical ways a crystal can change. If you handle it too roughly, it might break. It might chip or become eroded by contact with other stones in a pouch. But that's not really what I'm referring to here.

Another idea some folks have is that their crystals are growing over time or that it's even possible for that to happen. Crystals do all their growing underground where the chemical wash and circumstances are just so. It is impossible for a crystal to add layers or expand its size in your possession unless you are working in a laboratory setting that can somehow mimic the specific conditions your crystal would need to have grown naturally underground.

Stranger things have happened though, so I'll never say never. But it's safe to say that for the most part, what I say here is true.

6. ELIXIRS ARE NOT THE ULTIMATE DISTILLATION OF CRYSTAL ENERGY

Many people swear by crystal elixirs, where you soak crystals in water—or surround a sealed chamber holding crystals with drinking water—later to imbibe the imbued water. They're great. I've used them and I do believe they are special.

I've done blind taste tests with others and the crystal water really does feel different going down. I like that fine. But when faced with choosing an elixir over an actual stone, I'll always choose the stone itself. After all, the stone is the thing the elixir is trying to copy, which makes the original automatically preferable.

I also choose primarily to experience stones through my sense of touch and imagination, so I'd rather not be ingesting them. You never know what chemicals may have been used to tumble a stone, even if it's not known to be composed of any dangerous elements itself. It might have residue from processing or have been dyed or soaked in something you can't detect. There are other stones that will dissolve in water (Selenite) and still others that are actually poisonous (like Orpiment, or Arsenic Sulfide).

Yes, you can contain the stones separately from the water. That's the same process again, but once removed. It can work—but is it really worth it when picking up a stone is faster—and I think better.

SELF   IMAGE 30

AVENTURINE chunk (Brazil), more on page 122
At Home with the Self

7. **CRYSTALS AND GENDER** (NOT NECESSARILY A THING)

It might seem strange to you, or very comforting, to see stones as individuals. "She doesn't want to be held." Or, "He's hiding right now."

"They are the crystal people." I understand the temptation to anthropomorphize crystals. I do believe entities can reside in inanimate objects. But people are a unique and distinctive part of creation. So are the stones. Parallels and similarities should be embraced, but the two ought not to be equated as somehow the same.

I believe stones are discrete and mostly impersonal energy bundles (albeit connected to the vast universal matrix). Their individuality has to do with the uniqueness of that quality of vibration (or shape, or texture, etc.) and doesn't benefit or care about our projections of human qualities (be they through name, gender, or affections). Making them into little pets feels belittling. Do it if you must, but it's not prerequisite to my understanding of how crystals operate.

However, to build on my mention above, it is nonetheless possible for particular entities to take up residence in crystals and an awareness of that is helpful and important. I just don't think it's an all-the-time thing. And to be fair (and compassionate), if what I've disagreed with above floats your boat and allows your relationship with stones to bubble, then more power to ya! It's just not a necessary part of my understanding of crystals.

IMAGE 31   SELF

CITRINE, natural point (Brazil), more on page 123

The Positive Self

8. **CRYSTALS AREN'T PANACEAS** (NOTHING IS A CURE-ALL)

You may not have noticed this odd coincidence, but a casual perusal of any crystal book or online resource will trot out a litany of things that any given stone will do for you. Nothing wrong with that. What's surprising—and problematic—is that the next stone might have all the same qualities, only listed in a different order. I exaggerate a bit, but try it as an experiment. You'll quickly see what I'm talking about. Any given stone will be listed as calming yet exciting, grounding yet elevating. Read far enough into the text and it'll seem like any crystal could do everything any person could ever want or need for it to do.

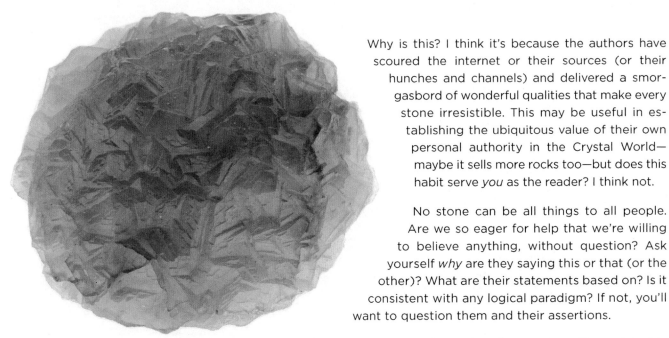

SELF   IMAGE 32

AMBER FLUORITE geometric cluster
(China), more on page 124

The Maturing Self

Why is this? I think it's because the authors have scoured the internet or their sources (or their hunches and channels) and delivered a smorgasbord of wonderful qualities that make every stone irresistible. This may be useful in establishing the ubiquitous value of their own personal authority in the Crystal World—maybe it sells more rocks too—but does this habit serve *you* as the reader? I think not.

No stone can be all things to all people. Are we so eager for help that we're willing to believe anything, without question? Ask yourself *why* are they saying this or that (or the other)? What are their statements based on? Is it consistent with any logical paradigm? If not, you'll want to question them and their assertions.

I'll be the first to tell you that I have not-readily-explainable elements to my stone attributions. For example, several energy zones each feature green stones. The reason for this is that color alone is not what I take into consideration.

Density, darkness, or lightness. Surfacing complexity. All these are relevant. It would take much longer to explain the placement of all the given stones into my paradigm than we have time or pages in this book to outline. You can always query me regarding attributions by contacting me directly.

What I will say is that my claims regarding one stone will not be identical to those for another. They each have their own significance and while there can be some overlap or similarities, no two stones deliver exactly the same thing in my system, however you choose to jumble their qualities. I consider this revolutionary, given the context of the existing crystal lore.

Also, and this is important, the same stone might deliver different qualities in different circumstances (like night vs. day). And it might react differently depending on the person using it. I see this all the time in how people report their experience of even the same type of stone in meditations.

It's for this reason that once you learn my paradigm and fine tune your own geo-sentience, you should break away from the experts (including myself) and come up with your own intuitive assessments of the stones. It's a great skill to have.

My wife tells a story from when we first met. She would ask me about a stone's qualities and I'd tell her to close her eyes and see what she came up with. Remarkably, it was often in tune with what I would have said!

9. BEWARE OF PRESCRIPTIONS (AN EASY FIX IS A FALSE PROMISE)

The medical model is prescriptive. "Take this for that." It offers a one-to-one solution or remedy.

On the most basic level, someone could say, "Such-and-such stone is good for the pineal gland." I respond, "Wait, do you even know what the pineal gland is (or does)?"

What is it about the stone that would make the pineal gland sing? If you can't answer that, you may be headed in the wrong direction. For energy healing to work best, it really helps if you're on board with a complete understanding of what's going on. You want to be clear about your expectations and what they are based on.

People ask me for a stone that will bring prosperity or love. The dynamics behind a person's love life or earning potential are far too complicated to be fixed with a finger snap. The reason one person is having difficulty with love may differ completely from what the next person is going through. One stone cannot hope to handily resolve the nuanced complexities of love and prosperity.

I reject the oversimplification that the prescriptive model offers.

Holistic health is all about looking at the whole person. To offer easy fixes is not ultimately holistic. We need to take the long view, the all-around view.

10. LABELS ARE IMPORTANT (BUYER BEWARE)

It often comes as a shock to people when I show them the difference between a true or natural Citrine and the heat-treated or baked Amethyst commonly sold as Citrine. They look different in formation and color. And one is way more rare (and expensive) than the other. Yet, 95% of vendors don't think twice about labeling the latter as Citrine, which it is not.

Likewise, many metaphysical resources will be sloppy about exposing these distinctions. I was particularly shocked to open up a best-selling

IMAGE 33   SELF

GOLDEN RUTILATED QUARTZ
cluster (Brazil), more on page 124
Spreading your Light

crystal book and find not one, but three photos of fake Citrine being showcased as the real thing. How seriously can we take a source like that, when they make one of the biggest rookie mistakes in the business?

As influencers, these authors should know better. But you can hardly blame them when vendors and big wholesalers, established for decades, routinely pass off fraudulently labeled items as being what they're not.

For example, Serpentine is pervasively sold as Jade, which it ain't. If you're going to use labels, make them accurate and descriptive! For example, I call Serpentines "Jade-like" or baked Amethyst "faux Citrine" (from the French word for fake). I'll even put "Citrine" alone in scare quotes, so people can be alerted to the difference and know what they're really getting. It's beautiful anyhow, so why lie about it? Especially because energetically, there's a very relevant difference between true Citrine and its facsimiles. Ditto with Jade. It's bad business and bad practice to mislabel, no matter how you look at it.

Let me touch on one more pet peeve. Too many plain Quartz crystals are sold as Lemurian Quartz. Labeling them as such does not make them so. Lemurians are Lemurians particularly because of their distinctive exterior crystallization (which other Quartzes lack). And yet routinely, random Quartzes are labeled as Lemurians by unscrupulous vendors to make easy sales to unsuspecting buyers. It's also annoying to see cut and polished pieces labeled as Lemurian, when the mere act of eliminating any natural surfacing automatically disqualifies a crystal from being identifiable as Lemurian.

I'm still stumped when it comes to identifying Jadeites, but there are gemologists with fancy instruments that can make the determination accurately. I've paid to have several stones appraised in this way. Sometimes it's worth investing the time or money to verify what the naked eye cannot.

What's a buyer to do? Educate yourself regarding the type of stone you're interested in. Talk to experts like myself. We're often happy to clarify any issues you might be having.

11. **NOTHING BUT *THIS* WILL DO!**

I can't tell you the number of times people have come into my store looking for something obscure because they were drawn to how it was described in some book. That pushes my buttons for several reasons. It's what I would call an over-attachment to labels. Let me explain.

While the comprehensiveness of some resources out there is admirable, several stones featured are simply not widely available. Having them in stock becomes a challenge for sellers like me. Take for example, Phenacite. It generally comes in expensively small crystals with poorly formed terminations. Stocking it for every 500th customer who might care about it is neither convenient nor affordable. Ditto Natrolite, Petalite, Herderite, or any number of other cult favorites. Still, I keep my eye out for them in case I find something decent enough to share at the right price.

I have an extremely wide range of products, but I feel blindsided when someone comes in specifically demanding that *one* type of stone I don't carry. They won't settle for anything else. Which brings up my second issue with some people's over-attachment to labels. If the customer could understand and express what they're *really* looking for—the underlying *quality* of the stone in question, whatever it was that drew them to it (instead of getting stuck on whatever they may have read somewhere)—there may be *plenty* of other, cheaper, and more abundant alternatives to choose from.

This happened in my shop recently, when someone came in looking for Cassiterite specifically. It's a great stone, quite rare, and I have personal pieces of it. Her phone was open to the site she'd learned about it on, and once I discovered what she was really looking for help with, we quickly found something easily available and affordably priced to suit her needs.

I recommend you have a look under the hood, move past the names and labels. Start always from your place of need. It's from there that the best options will present themselves.

12. QUESTIONS, MEET THE ANSWERS

A recurrent theme of this book is the inquiry and how important it is, because it helps you get to the root of the problem or issue that you're grappling with. What I want to address in this section, which I don't see happen nearly enough from my experience in the Crystal World, is having people close the loop between question and answer.

We've become very accepting of open-ended questioning. We're told to question authority but not why or to what effect. We're told to question the mainstream media but not the society that created it or the superstructures that benefit from our supposed misinformation.

We turn to Google to answer all types of questions, quick and easy. I've often been written to by people who don't introduce themselves—

IMAGE 35   SELF

DARK PETRIFIED WOOD (AL, USA), more on page 126

Worldly Motion

where they're contacting me from, how they've heard of me (it's just rude)—demanding an identification for a stone or my response to some random question they have. I am not a search bar. I'm old school that way.

I guess the myth I'm trying to bust here is the myth of instant, easy, and thorough answers. Try as you might, you really can't expect to get all three at the same time. You may get quick answers, but they won't necessarily be accurate.

Also, I want to address a variation on this theme which some folks might not notice, but I see it all the time. That variation is the question that gets asked with no regard for the actual answer. There *is* an answer, and it *does* matter. But for some reason, they never intended to actually hear or learn from that answer. Other times people hear it, but they don't retain it or seem to really care what it is. This gives me pause. For example, someone asks about what a wand is but doesn't really want to know. Alternatively, they might not comprehend its function, even if it is explained to them.

What I'm advocating for here—to bust both the easy-answer myth *and* the "I don't actually care what the answer is" instinct—is that you really consider the meaning and implications of your questions *before* asking them. The solution to this problem rests with you. I recommend that you understand why your question matters, inquire respectfully—providing context—and prepare yourself to actually hear (and retain) what's said in response. This way you can close the loop more successfully between all questions and answers.

SELF   IMAGE 36

LIGHT PETRIFIED WOOD (Madagascar), more on page 126

Acting on the World

13. **CREDENTIALS SHMEDENTIALS** (WHO'S REALLY THE BOSS?)

We live in an iconoclastic time. Authority has lost its luster. You can find experts supporting views from anywhere on the spectrum. So whose opinion or assertions do you trust?

I don't believe that letters (degrees, certifications, and titles) automatically confer bragging rights. I've seen people get them (and flaunt them) with the expectation that we should all bow down out of respect for those laurels, rather than in honor of the quality of their character, or the content of their true knowledge.

I don't do that. It matters more to me what you're saying and why, not simply what qualifications you can claim. Lived experience can teach you more than a restricted course of study. Although valuable, it's what you do with your credentials that matters most.

Doctors will freely admit that there are other, terrible doctors out there who've still earned degrees, and are licensed to practice in spite of the lesser quality of their care. What makes a great doctor is not just their training, but what they are willing to learn from their actual practice in the field. Heart and compassion go a long way to making you a truly outstanding practitioner in any field.

Someone I know said, "I'm a certified crystal healer" as an unsolicited rebuttal for why they didn't need to study with me. My lesser self heard their statement as a personal attack. I was like, "Excuse me!?" But on reflection, I learned something important from the interaction—that people choose and identify with their mentors. This is great, but it can also result in them having blinders on to other good people and completely credible (and possibly competing) ideas.

The Crystal World and New Age thinking can be confusing enough to navigate without having to give everyone the time of day. Ultimately, we do have to decide who to follow, who to give the most credence to. I just recommend that you not lose your curiosity. Everyone has a little something to contribute to your understanding.

I hope this book will contribute a lot to your own knowledge and comprehension. I'd like it to open some new wings of thought in the Crystal World. Having a whole new audience consider my perspectives will stretch what people are looking for and finding from their teachers (and from the crystals themselves!).

IMAGE 37   SELF

Psilomelane (Mexico), more on page 127
Connecting Aspects of the Self

Ultimately, you're the boss of your own learning process and practice.

14. **INVOKING TRADITIONS** (IT'S NOT THE HOLY GRAIL)

Occasionally, mavens of the Crystal World invoke science to validate their beliefs. It's great to find supportive cross-parallels, but you won't have to look far to find a scientist who'll trash our belief in the power of stones. If it's not verifiable through rigorous testing, it seems pointless to even go there for any kind of a comprehensive scientific anchor or validation of crystal healing.

Others invoke ancient traditions, shamanic lineages—the wisdom of lost civilizations (Atlantis, Lemuria), or even the Pleiades (the Seven Sisters star cluster)—as a pedigree to prove the authenticity of their beliefs. I have trouble with all that. Given the lack of accurate records or accounts from any one of these sources, I find it sketchy for people to claim with any certainty that this or that is what those societies believed (or practiced).

Humility is key. Be wary of anyone who assures you they have it all figured out. An openness to learn or to be shown new understandings over time is important. I've learned some major lessons just this year. For three decades I had discounted plain old rocks like the type you'd find in your driveway. Now I revere them and have added them to my energy zone system as Bedrock, Foundation stones.

I look forward to continuing my learning in the future. There are so many stones whose energies I'm looking forward to understanding better. Just 'cause I've figured out an enormous amount, doesn't mean I have it *all* figured out.

My beliefs are firmly founded on my personal and collective experience, including those of my clients and students. I teach from that place, but don't accept my own words unthinkingly. Match them with your own understanding in order to recognize whether or not what I'm saying makes sense with how you're feeling and where you want to go with your own crystal practice.

SELF   IMAGE 38

PYRITE, octahedral cluster (Peru), more on page 127

Owning Your Space, Protector of Self

Yes, I've inferred that my knowledge comes from alien sources, which I certainly cannot prove to you. But if you take my word for it—or embrace my teachings, much as you would any teacher's—let its resonance with (and inside) of you be its primary proof of legitimacy.

What I'm saying is that stories and inspirational wellsprings are all well and good, but they are not themselves proof of anything. The proof, as they say, is in the pudding.

15. **SPIRIT LEADS YOU** (NOT SO FAST)

Many people are driven by intuition, and that's great. I've seen people pick their crystals based on what their spirit guides say. I do believe forces beyond our control bring into our lives the various stones we have to work with.

However, I'm not willing to give up my decision-making entirely to Spirit or to believe that reason, logic, and responsibility are somehow strangers to Spirit.

I knew someone who claimed Spirit runs everything, and I'm willing to accept that—to a point. What I object to is my sense that when we give up our own volition to a higher power, we either abdicate responsibility for our actions or end up just serving *ourselves* in the name of Spirit.

Do you know anyone like that? They back out of a plan you've made with them last minute because Spirit told them to. They didn't buy something they wanted because their pendulum said it wasn't okay. It's nice if you and Spirit (or you and your pendulum) are that closely tied, but it doesn't inspire confidence in me to count on you keeping your word when it's dependent on something outside of you, that's so mutably intangible.

The Enlightenment—and a lot of the major religions, if you check them out—place a lot of stock in free will and choice.

IMAGE 39   SELF

GOLDEN SCHEELITE octrahedral crystal (China), more on page 128

The Highest Self

The metaphysical world is very important, but so is the practical world. My goal in straddling both is to do so with balance.

My bottom line, as far as the crystals are concerned, is to own it. Understand why you do or don't want a certain stone, why you will or won't take a certain action. Don't give up your power, your own sense of choice, and your responsibility.

That's a recurrent theme in this book, if you haven't noticed already. Research, look within, but ultimately own your perspective. Base it on something solid. Whether real or imagined, just give yourself a good anchor.

16. ALL IS NOT LIGHT

There is an idea very prevalent in the Crystal World and across the modalities of New Age thought. It's what I consider to be an obsession with, even an idolatry of, "The Light." People sign their communications, "In Love and Light." People refer to themselves as Light Workers.

This is all well and good, but it seems to ignore the fact that half of each day (as well as all of outer space) is shrouded in darkness. In our culture, casual conversations will use terms like "being in a dark mood" or "he has a dark side of him." I think that's wrong and harmful.

I understand the need to make distinctions, but this feels like a false dichotomy. Nature exists in a delicate state of balance, constantly seeking equilibrium. The slightest tip of the scales can ruin entire ecosystems. Too much light can be dangerous, too much dark can be dangerous. The seasons swap daytime for nighttime as we travel between the equinoxes.

It's all good. What I recommend is that we find the balance in both, often using one or the other to find that place of harmony we seek. For example, you can find shade on a hot day or use a flashlight to see in the dark.

How does this play out with crystals? For starters, in the Channel Energy Zone (where I've placed most of the black and white stones), dark and light stones are roughly equal in number. They don't necessarily represent diametric or incompatible opposites. One might represent boundaries, another open channels. You can use and embrace both of them.

As a child, I had times when I was afraid of the dark. Sometimes there are good reasons for us to fear a condition where we cannot fully use our senses and we're unable to tell what's out there. That's understandable.

The absence of light can and should be accepted as being okay—not less than, or frowned upon, relative to the light. People equate light with life itself and darkness with death. But as you'll see in my system, black stones have several vital, life-affirming functions such as defining, clearing, or opening space. The black and the dark can (and should be) our friend, just as readily as the light.

SELF   IMAGE 40

SUPER SEVEN pendant, type 1 (Brazil), more on page 128

Hailing Multiple Sources

UNDERSTANDING CRYSTALS

In Part One, I told my story and differentiated myself in a few dozen ways. Here in Part Two, I will present to you my 10 Energy Zone system, outline the various concepts needed to better understand crystals, and describe how to work with them through eight primary life challenges and phases. This will help you make the most sense of the reference listings in Part Three.

The 10 Energy Zone System

This system is like the central artery or highway running through a city. The concepts featured above and below are all like the on-and-off ramps that make the traffic move more easily. Our guiding light is the subtitle of this book: "Understanding and Working with Crystals for Clarity and Flow."

FROM CHAKRAS TO ENERGY ZONES

As I was seeking a way to systematize my knowledge of crystals, I stumbled on the chakra paradigm from ancient India. It allows us to understand the entire scope of human experience through a series of energy centers that swirl around various vortexes on our physical person.

Here's a list of the traditional chakras (and where they're located on the body):

1. Root (base of the torso)
2. Sacral (just below the navel)
3. Solar Plexus (where the ribs come together)
4. Heart (in line with the heart)
5. Throat (neck)
6. Third Eye (forehead, above and between the eyes)
7. Crown (head-top)

I won't say more about the chakras here because so much has already been written about them "out there." My focus is on how we put them to use with the crystals.

What you'll see in the diagram below—and through my various explanations—is that I've renamed the chakras as Energy Zones, added three new ones, and changed the interpretation (and title) of some others.

THE HUMAN/CRYSTAL ENERGY ZONE DIAGRAM

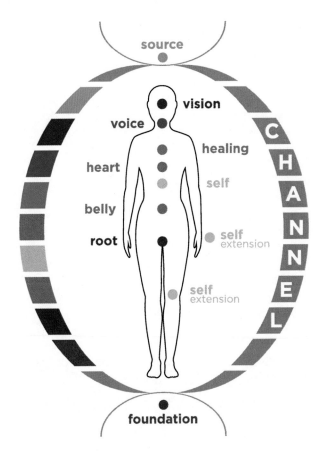

Foundation

Foundation precedes Root and is located below the body, physically and metaphorically. It has to do with what came before us, in terms of ancestry and prehistoric life in general (plant and animal). It also concerns the layers of this life, like the rings of a tree, which immortalize an organism's growth over the years (and tells tales of both hardship and flourishing). Lastly, it refers to the bedrock, the earth itself that we are rooted into and grounded by. This is the physical foundation from which we came, and to which we return.

Stones that are relevant to this give us a physical reminder of it because they're fossilized creatures or vegetation, or even just layered and weathered remnants of geological time. They connect us to personal and family history and help us to work on some of the issues which may have arisen through the challenges we or they may have faced.

Root

Root includes the sacral chakra for me, which I never thought was meaningfully different from root. It's at the base of the torso and is the place where we connect with the earth, going from antecedent or pre-being into taking physical form. It has to do with reproduction, arousal, and pleasure, all of which are ideally built on a sense of safety and the celebration of life.

IMAGE 41   SELF

TIGER EYE faceted palm piece (Brazil),
more on page 129

Positive Reflection on the Self

This zone has its own unique form of blockages, stemming from people's discomfort or maladjustment to their sexuality (or even their physical existence). It is the point on the body furthest from the head and most easily waylaid by over-intellectualization. Sexual trauma is often lodged here, even though its impacts can be felt in other energy zones like Self.

The stones we use here are for grounding, feeling connected to and safe with the earth. People for whom being in their body has felt dangerous are sometimes dissociated from it and this energy zone. By connecting to the planet and using some of the other stones that interface between us and Foundation, we can rebuild a sense of trust. An important part of that is rekindling, allowing, and welcoming life force, and the idea of cellular regeneration, which comes from a positive (not self-destructive) relationship with our body.

Belly

Belly replaces any part of the sacral chakra that isn't already addressed by the Root zone. It circulates around the navel. If you put both hands onto your belly, with the navel in the middle, that's where I'm talking about. It includes the digestive system and all the organs of the torso. This zone speaks to our internal process, not just how we digest our meals but also how we fight infection, deal with food poisoning, any illness of the

body. It isn't vocal, it doesn't speak. It operates with great autonomy and pre-programmed, instinctive wisdom.

We have to trust our gut (belly) and give it proper fuel. With food and body issues abounding in this day and age, our relationship to this powerhouse has often become somewhat fraught and in need of its very own type of healing. I have a relatively small number of stones directly associated with this area. They support our tuning into it, visualizing parts of it, soothing it, and working with its enormous transformative potential.

HEART   IMAGE 42

BLOODSTONE large chunk (India), more on page 131

Self in Community

Self

Self replaces solar plexus, still located at the sternum, where your ribs come together. It has to do with (and there are particular stones associated with) things like your positive ego or originally unsullied self, the way it was or could be despite any acquired insecurities. It also concerns healthy personal pride and boundaries, standing our ground. Self is connected to personal growth, breaking out of your shell, getting out of your own way. It has to do with how you see yourself, warts and all, and what standards you hold yourself to when aspiring to achieve fulfillment and become your own best self. There are many ways we can get off track in this zone and our relationship with it can be damaged by bullying and abuse, which take their toll all up and down the entire energy system.

Heart

Heart is in the middle of the chest, it is the feeling center of our being. Interestingly, the stones I've attributed to it have the widest spread in terms of colors, from the traditional green and pink to milky white and translucent brown. Concepts like forgiveness, compassion, and nurturance have a home here. This is where we work on making it hospitable for these energies to thrive. A closed heart, a broken heart, a heavy heart—these are all symptoms of trouble that can show up here, including unaddressed emotions, anger, resentment, feeling alone, abandoned. There's always plenty of work to be done in the Heart Energy Zone.

Healing

I created the Healing Zone because I'd identified a host of stones that are connected to alignment and realignment, some with salutary effects on other zones. They needed a home on the body and the chest or lungs made sense to me as the right spot for them to live.

We connect to the outside world in many ways, but our breathing is the ultimate symbol of that give and take, the ebb and flow that resembles the ceaseless crashing of waves on every shore. It is by maintaining the balance between our inside and outside that our health is ultimately sustained. When we are unwell, we have to fight to regain that sense of balance and normality.

We cough from our lungs in a violent attempt to expel what ails us. While total restoration of health may not always be possible, the stones associated with this zone can help us embrace both our weaknesses and strengths, and focus on the places we want to work on for our ongoing wellness.

Voice

Voice replaces throat, which seemed mostly to speak to its location. I'm now using a word that symbolizes actualization, the process by which thoughts are formed into words and then spoken. This also is the process of manifestation, when an idea is transformed into reality. It's very important that we find our voice and use it, whether in relationships, at work, or even politically. There is a stone for each of these various dynamics. There are also stones that help us listen to how we speak to ourselves and others with compassion and gentleness. Being silenced or afraid to speak up creates a myriad of problems, as does speaking too much and too loudly (over other people). Voice is one of the ways we modulate our relationship with the self and other people.

Vision

Vision replaces in name the third eye chakra, again my effort to move away from simply identifying a location (center of the forehead), instead exploring the concept of what it means to *be* in this energy zone. Vision can be inward or outward, down-ward or upward. It's the ideally vibrant home of innovation,

IMAGE 43   HEART

EMERALD relationship stone cluster (Brazil), more on page 131

Deeper Love

creativity, imagination, and the subconscious. There are stones that represent all these dynamics. It is also where we conceive of and pursue our own spiritual mission, or purpose in life.

Having blinders on, lacking originality, being bored, boxed in—these are all enemies of Vision. It takes fortitude, focus, and control to open this Pandora's box of access to the subconscious, the underworld, and the Dreamtime. So much becomes possible if you tap into your sense of vision with openness and intelligent curiosity.

HEART   IMAGE 44

NEPHRITE JADE tumbler (Canada), more on page 132

Embrace of Mother Earth

Source

Source can be associated with the crown chakra, but again, it's not limited to a location on your body. In fact, it's slightly elevated, at the interface where we (including our aura) ends, and the Universal begins. As Root and Foundation act as connection points to the earth, Source is our connection point for the heavens or ascension. It is how we interface with our spirit guides, angels, G8D, and the divine. Vision is the vehicle, and Source is the destination. It is heaven. It is where our ancestors and descendants meet, where the self communes with the All.

People who lack vision and/or are disconnected from Source, have trouble connecting with this level of being and the many splendors it offers. They may feel spiritually bereft, abandoned, alone in the world. I believe Source is where we can best access our sense of meaning, relevance, and spiritual connection in this life.

Channel

Here we are no longer connected to the body. We are dealing with how the flow of energy is modulated, facilitated, or managed in general (or specifically). When I speak of Channel, I'm talking about dynamics like an automatically open conduit, clearing a path, creating boundaries, having a guardian, an attack dog, even a sculptural representation of yourself, an animal, other people or even deities. Many stones step up to represent these functions. Interestingly—apart from the general stone-carving category—many are black or white in color. Therapeutically, they can be used to install better protections, access higher planes, or remove barriers. People who experience blockages and any number of other issues can supplement the work they do with the other energy zone stones by using Channel stones to move and manage energy.

Choosing Crystals

Now that we've outlined the ten Energy Zones, look for them to show up in this section strategically, as I lay out for you various crystal concepts, forms, placements, and details regarding how to use crystals for life.

COLLECTING CRYSTALS

There are several ways for you to acquire crystals. Perhaps one of the most respected methods is to go prospecting for them yourself. There are many rockhounds out there who'll be happy to show you the ropes and there are plenty of gem and mineral clubs around to join. I was part of one myself for a time. I also mined (or hammered) for Herkimer Diamonds with my kids when they were young. It's thankless work, but last time we went, we were inspired by an old master doing his thing. He knew exactly where to hack the big chunks to reveal some tasty inner pockets. It's not easy, but it can be rewarding and if you're bitten by the bug, that's a great way to go.

You can also go to museums, where the most outstanding discoveries ever made are being housed behind glass. It's awesome (literally) to see them, but too bad we can't touch them in that context. Plus, museum shops don't tend to have the most wonderful selections of crystals for purchase, being generally tourist traps.

IMAGE 45   HEART

KUNZITE crystal (Pakistan), more on page 132

Higher Love

If you're just window shopping, Pinterest is a great way to go. I once did a whole webinar on searching for and organizing your virtual collection of crystal images on Pinterest. There are extraordinary specimens to be seen there, which makes it a great resource for learning as well. Regrettably, the descriptions are often absent or not fleshed out as much as they might be.

Next, there's your local rock shop. If you're lucky, you might stumble across one by chance on a road trip. I've been known to make dedicated trips and detours just to check out certain places I've heard of. You always find something you've never seen anywhere else at a crystal store, and these folks need your business. As a small business person myself, I respect and like to support these mineral oases. And of course, I appreciate the patrons who frequent my own shop.

A big challenge for small shops is maintaining a diverse inventory. It's expensive to have a huge selection, and you're at a disadvantage when the public can just type something into their search bar and get the entire internet's backstock to choose from. That's the power of the web.

Online you can search for just about anything and most likely find it. For people who prefer to pick their stones in person, this can be unattractive. Also, size, color, and authenticity can be misrepresented online. This makes the internet a mixed blessing, not least of which because it's been chipping away at the role and stability of brick and mortar mom-and-pop shops.

Lastly, you have gem, mineral, and fossil shows. They come up a few times a year, depending on where you live. The biggest one in the world (by far) happens in Tucson, Arizona every January/February. It actually consists of up to 50 slightly staggered but mostly simultaneous shows. What's attractive about these is that you often see vendors coming right from the source: Mexicans, Peruvians, Moroccans, Chinese, the list goes on and on.

If you're easily overwhelmed, these events might not be for you, because they are absolutely overwhelming. You'll have FOMO and hold off, only to find that thing (or vendor) you wanted to get back to has been lost in the hullabaloo. Or you'll buy something you're excited about only to find that someone else has it for cheaper, or a better specimen. Unless you can stick to a very tight budget, just as you would going into a casino, I think these shows are best navigated by the pros.

HEART   IMAGE 46

LEPIDOLITE hearts (Brazil),
more on page 133

True Intimacy

I straddle these worlds because I have a shop. I go to these shows and I'm a vendor at these shows too. My selection has to be competitive with direct importers, wholesalers, and retail chains. I focus on quality over quantity, going deep into many varieties with an uncommon selection. I also offer what I call quality custom crystal mail order remotely. I go the extra mile of taking additional photos and videos to help folks choose what's exactly right for them. It's nice to have someone advise you regarding metaphysical qualities without having to reference any books. It's like providing the best of both worlds, as close to shopping in person as you can get.

"WHICH STONE SHOULD I BUY?"

This is an age-old question. I hear it all the time, "How do I choose what crystal to get?"

You can choose what you're drawn to or, based on your references (or your friend or mentor), what you or they think would be good for you. It can sometimes be a bit like choosing food. Ideally, those two would be the same, what you need and what you want. Think: choosing a nutritious meal over one that's simply tasty.

IMAGE 47   HEART

MALACHITE display piece (Congo),
more on page 134

Feel your Feelings

One thing I can tell you from making thousands of sales is that nine times out of ten, people go for what attracts them personally over any other consideration. For many people, particularly if they're newer to it, that's whatever's glittery and pretty. Cheap doesn't hurt either.

As you learn more and your interests deepen, you will find yourself drawn to stones for their rarity or unusual qualities, visual or otherwise. You'll find yourself spending more as you start to recognize the truly outstanding specimens. In short, the answer to this question of which stone you should buy will evolve over time.

What follows are many more criteria for you to consider when making your choices. These will also help you actually put your crystals to use. You'll want to use this and other resources to identify and keep track of what you have. More than a few folks I know have amassed huge collections, but hardly remember the names of many of their crystals, never mind their qualities.

Crystal Forms

ROUGH VERSUS POLISHED

Some folks are purists. They refuse to work with anything that's been polished or modified. News for them, the mere fact that crystals are out of the ground and available for purchase means they've been modified from their original state. Had they been left as they were, they'd still be in the ground.

Still, it's possible to limit your collection to stones that have been found (like on a beach), not mined or broken in any way. That's certainly respectable. It just drastically limits what material you have to work with.

HEART   IMAGE 48

MILKY QUARTZ soft cut tabular point (Brazil), more on page 134

Compassion and Nurturance

That being said, I share a preference for some stones rough over polished. Lemurian Quartzes for example, their main claim to fame is their distinctive exterior siding and termination structure. Cut that off and what have you got? A Quartz like any other. Moldavite also derives most of its uniqueness from its intricate surfacing. And yet, faceted Moldavite has a charm all its own too.

There are some stones I prefer polished. Take Rose Quartz, for example. Chunks are nice to have around, but the polishing gives you easier access to the energy within. Sugilite is beautiful when polished—and polishing often makes stones more amenable to jewelry—but there's nothing like the rough (for me) in terms of feeling Sugilite energy.

I could go on forever with my preferences regarding which stones are "better" rough than polished, or vice versa, but I mostly wanted to introduce you to the distinction and highlight that it's different for different stones and certainly changes from person to person.

COLOR, PATTERN, TEXTURE, AND DENSITY

Color, pattern, and texture are huge considerations when choosing crystals—and they vary widely from stone to stone. For example, when there's more black than green in Malachite, it's heavier and deeper in vibration (more grounding). But the most valuable and spectacular display pieces have vivid patterns and are more green than black.

Sometimes it's the color within that matters most to people. Moldavite often appears black until you put a light through it. Then it's either a dark olive, electric green, or even neon green (they call that color "poison"). Rhodochrosite is most prized when it's a rich, dark, and translucent red, but there's a price trade-off, as the softer pinks are more affordable (and plentiful).

Pattern is a dominant consideration in a number of stones. Agates and Jaspers, for example, have what I call 2D (two-dimensional) patterns and offer a staggering variety of distinctive visuals. Seraphinite and Charoite are other stones for which there is not nearly as much variety of types, but I call them 3D (three-dimensionally) patterned. That quality makes all the difference between an A-grade specimen (less fancy design with foreign material inclusions) and a AAA-grade specimen (where it's all green or purple and with vibrantly chatoyant patterning consistently throughout). Labradorite, Sheen Obsidian, and Tiger Eye are other good examples of 3D patterning.

Texture comes also in a stone's surface, which can be felt and visually observed. By feel, I mean what does the surface feel like when you touch or rub it? Lapis and Sugilite can go from gritty to waxy in feel, waxy being a great deal more rare and valuable. Calcite is often acid washed to go from flaky to smooth. Polished Lepidolite and river worn Jade's softness resembles the touch of human skin.

Differently, there are whole classes of stones whose intricate surfacing are their primary attraction. Nirvana Quartz, Tektites, Elestial Quartz, and etched stones in general come to mind. I think of them like the endless surface area of the human brain or a delicately jagged shoreline. There's more surface area, ultimately,

IMAGE 49   HEART

"FOREST JADE" SERPENTINE polished boulder (Pakistan), more on page 135

Almost There

than a smooth face, because of all the nooks and crannies. And just like an English muffin, there are more connection points for flavor. Or as in the case of the human mind, more potential contacts for neuro-electrical transmissions that enhance the layers and complexity of thought, knowledge, and wisdom.

Weight, relative to size, can play an important role in your experience of crystals. Hematite or Meteorites nail you down fast with their dense metallic gravity. Celestite is a great example of a stone with contrasting features—the light celestial blue takes you up into the ethers while the weighty crystal and matrix brings you right down to earth, evoking a sense of movement like the precipitation of rain from on high, falling down to the surface.

To the contrary, some stones are deceptively light compared to how they look. And this is a valuable quality too. It has less density than what's around it, enabling it metaphorically to lift blockage by (and here I'm using the word unusually) osmosis. I'm speaking of Amber, Jet, and Snowy Carnelian. They all have this quality of being strangely light, enabling them to metaphysically loosen obstructions.

BIGGER PIECES VERSUS SMALLER PIECES

To the question of whether or not size matters, the answer is that it depends on what you do with it. It's like with pendants. I prefer larger ones while some people prefer smaller ones. Also relevant are the stone's intrinsic qualities. Take for example the Moldavite that catapulted me into the Crystal World, it was small. As I've said in presentations and to customers, particularly about Moldavite, a tray of them can be like a tray of cell phones. One might lead to the corner pizza guy and one might lead to the head of some faraway galaxy. There are no easy answers. As always, it depends.

HEART   IMAGE 50

"NEW JADE" SERPENTINE standing "perfumer" (China), more on page 135

Accessible Divine Love

All the above having been said, there are some applications that call specifically for small stones—particularly 3rd Eye pieces. In order to be placed on your forehead, they have to fit just so, and not fall off. Conversely, and people often ask me about this, to condition a healing or living room, or to put under your practitioner's treatment table, you'll need a substantial (ideally multi-pound) display piece. You have to match the stone to the space or the job required.

NATURAL CRYSTALLIZATIONS

1. Laser

Diamantina Quartz (named after its place of origin, in Brazil) is the classic all-natural laser point. It starts wider at the bottom and tapers steadily toward the tip where, almost as an after-thought, little termination facets complete the point. It acts as an automatic funnel, shuttling energy through and out of its point.

Many Lemurian Quartzes may act as lasers too. Almost any point can be used as a wand, I explain wands further in the next section. There are rare Red Laser Quartz and Edenite Quartz points from Madagascar that look almost identical to the Diamantina crystals.

IMAGE 11 **Edenite laser Quartz** page 15

IMAGE 18 **Red Laser Quartz** page 22

IMAGE 150 **Diamantina laser Quartz** page 157

IMAGE 171 **Lemurian laser** page 180

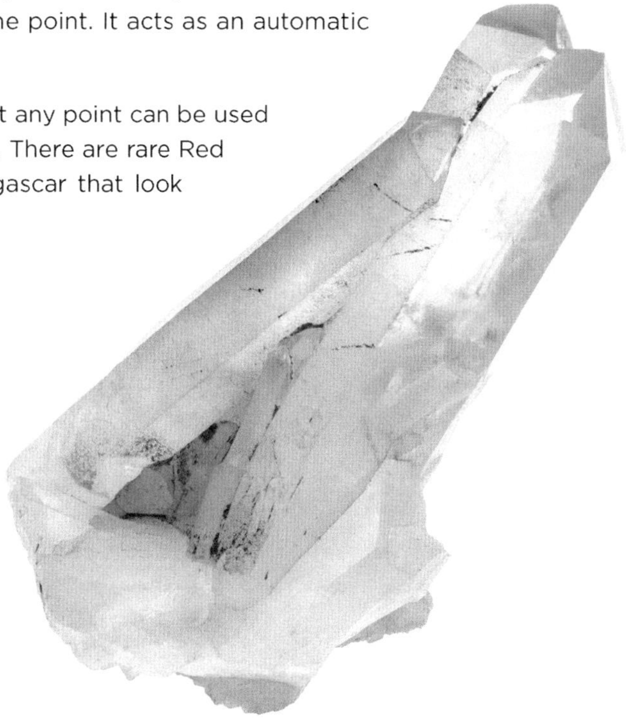

IMAGE 51 HEART

PINK QUARTZ relationship stones transmitter (Madagascar), more on page 59 + 136

Rose Tinted Glasses

2. Double Terminated

Generally longer than they are wide, these crystals (abbreviated DTs) are often reproduced in polished form. They come to a point at each end. They can push energy out each side, or they can shuttle that energy back and forth within. Which way you choose for them to operate is up to you, but somewhat dictated by the stone's shape. Longer makes it more a projector of energy while shorter lends itself better to being an internal energy generator (what I call a battery crystal, described next).

IMAGE 151 double terminated (**DT**), standing **Black Tourmaline** battery crystal page 158

IMAGE 155 **DT Quartz transmitter** page 162

IMAGE 156 **DT self-healed Citrine** page 163

HEART   IMAGE 52

ROSE QUARTZ large sphere (Madagascar), more on page 69 + 136

Unconditional Love

3. Battery

A battery crystal may be double terminated, but that's not required. The key is for it to be somewhat squat and internally oriented (i.e. not elongated). Almost literally, they can be the shape of a C or D battery. There's a fine distinction between "just a point" and a battery crystal. Battery crystals are a bit beefier and meant less to transmit energy than they are to hold and generate it.

IMAGE 151 **Black Tourmaline** battery crystal page 159

4. Tabular

Tabular crystals are just that, little tables that are usually rectangular and terminated at one or more ends. They hold and create space, lending themselves well to being a platform on which you can rest other stones. It is quite uncommon to find a tabular crystal, but you'll know it when you do!

Faden Quartz forms almost exclusively in tabular form, flat on each side, but often with too many intersecting segments to be exclusively tabular. Tabulars are nice to have as a novelty but are the least energetically versatile among the dozen forms highlighted here.

IMAGE 74 **Herkimer Diamond**, presenting like a tabular crystal page 80

IMAGE 152 unusual, vertically formed **Faden Quartz** crystal cluster page 159

5. Floater / Starburst

A double terminated, battery, or even a tabular crystal can be a floater. The key is that it be terminated all around, essentially formed "in solution" (in the wash of chemicals and temperatures that allow for crystallization in the ground). If you're a perfectionist, you'll want a floater to show no signs of attachment or breakpoints from a cluster or matrix. In theory, they are found loosely, lying around in the ground (or in a geode, vug, or cavity in the rock around them) near other same-type crystals. A favorite floater shape for me is the starburst, where the crystals shoot off in all directions.

Floaters are special for two reasons. First, they are that much more rare than even double terminated crystals. They are prized for that reason. And energetically, they're more integral, complete unto themselves. And yet they act as automatic generators, affecting their surrounding areas more than most simple crystal points.

IMAGE 55 starburst **Amethyst Flower** page 61

IMAGE 153 starburst **Blue Crystallized Quartz** page 160

6. Beta Quartz

You can buy cut stones (if you look) in this shape, but I'm more interested in how it occurs naturally. Beta Quartz has six three-sided pyramids coming together on the top, and six three-sided pyramids coming together identically on the bottom. These floaters are almost a level up from the octahedron, discussed later, and the fact that they occur naturally is mind blowing.

I have only been able to find very small complete Betas (from Siberia or Indonesia). Even cut and polished versions of this form are hard to find. Mostly, you see the underside started, but not completed, when it occurs naturally in a cluster.

IMAGE 154 **Beta Quartz** from China page 161

IMAGE 53   HEART

SMOKY QUARTZ heart (Madagascar),
more on page 137

Forgiveness, De-Toxification

7. Transmitter

In natural clusters, particularly among Quartzes, crystals tend to shoot off to the side and rarely straight up. When broken off, or even as free standing crystals, they may continue to stand in that same position, pointing off at a 45'ish degree angle. The value here is that they are naturally set up to send and receive energy, making them ideal for distance communication, healing, and the long range transmission of intention. All of the transmitters featured on these pages are natural and uncut or polished.

IMAGE 29 large cathedralized **Ametrine** transmitter page 33

IMAGE 51 pink **Madagascar Quartz** transmitter / Relationship Stone page 57

IMAGE 130 **Spirit Quartz** transmitter page 136

IMAGE 155 **DT Quartz** transmitter page 162

8. Cluster

Groups of more than a few points are called clusters. In Quartz, they point in all different directions, often making them handy to place spheres on. But energetically—aside from being beautiful, or maybe conditioning a room if they're particularly milky, frosty, or clear—that explicit multi-directionality feels disorganized. In Amethyst, the crystals tend to all point generally in the same direction (up), which makes those clusters more harmonious and recommended for conditioning a healing or treatment room. Oddly, Smoky Quartz (unless it's irradiated plain Quartz) and true Citrine are rarely found in clusters (or even pairs), making those occurrences particularly rare and valuable.

HEALING   IMAGE 54

AMBER freeform display piece (Chiapas, Mexico), more on page 139
Lifting Blockage

I've listed a host of different Quartz cluster occurrences, but other stones form in clusters too, like Apophyllite, Stilbite, and many others. Clusters are wonderful display pieces and, like I said, they're quite nice to set the energetic tone of a room. This is true even if the goal is purely aesthetic, in placement on a mantlepiece or coffee table.

IMAGE 10 red **Dragon Quartz** cluster page 14

IMAGE 56 **Lavender Amethyst** cluster page 62

IMAGE 62 **Milky Calcite** cluster page 68

IMAGE 71 large **Danburite** cluster page 77

IMAGE 73 **Pink Fluorite** cluster page 79

IMAGE 119 **Green Fluorite** cluster with record keepers page 126

IMAGE 133 **Aqua Aura Quartz** cluster page 140

9. Self-Healed

Most of the loose crystals you'll find are broken off from a base or cluster and look a bit like broken glass on one end. Some crystals may have had that happen in the ground but, because of still being awash in their chemicals and circumstances of origin, they were able to seal up that breakage with little jagged or broadly smooth re-crystallization.

These unusual crystals are called self-healed, which has obvious metaphorical value for those of us overcoming trauma and breakage in our own lives. It's encouraging and inspiring for us to imagine that we too can recover, sealing up our own wounds and scars to become a new kind of whole again.

IMAGE 156 self-healed **DT Citrine** page 163

10. Record Keepers and Trigons

Record Keepers are raised upward-pointing triangles that appear on a crystal face. I call the crystal face one of the natural "facets" at the tip of a crystal point (also often triangular). They're "outies" as such, since they stick up and out. Conversely, if they're indented (also known as trigons, and often pointing downward) I call them "innies." Pursuing the belly button analogy, people attribute these to being sort of umbilical cords to other places or higher knowledge, such as the Akashic Records. The Akashic Records are a New Age concept referring to everything that is, was, or will be. Anyone who knows what a record keeper is, generally treasures them as quite special. Although almost exclusively appearing on Quartz, I do reference a Fluorite below that has quite an extraordinary forest of record keepers on it.

IMAGE 119 **Green Fluorite** cluster coated with record keepers page 126

IMAGE 157 face of a **Nirvana Quartz**, coated with record keepers page 165

IMAGE 55   HEALING

AMETHYST FLOWER starburst cluster
(Brazil), more on page 140

Lasting Love

11. Trigonic Stones

Apart from trigons, we have trigonic stones that feature prominent and recurrent triangles that point one way and/or another. While not as rare as the traditional trigons and record keepers, these stones carry a similar weight or significance for those of us who imbue the triangle and pyramid with particular value and meaning. Besides our featured example in Ruby, one could argue that the cathedral Quartzes are also trigonic.

IMAGE 158 trigonic **Ruby crystal** page 166

12. Octahedrons

Let's talk about pyramidal triangles. You're going to really have to use your mind's eye here. I've done my best to explain everything in words—and we do have a photo to help with your visualization—but it's a good exercise to use these words to imagine the shapes I'm talking about.

Although made famous in ancient Egypt and Central America, the upward-pointing simple pyramid is a powerful shape. It has a grounded (four-sided) base along its bottom. And it has an arching point toward the heavens, consisting of four adjoining, perfect triangles.

HEALING   IMAGE 56

LAVENDER AMETHYST cluster (Brazil), more
on page 60 + 140

Spiritual Cleansing

Imagine the energies, more dispersed from below, converging up from the earth towards the apex of the pyramid (and beaming up to the heavens). Conversely, envision beams of light or astral energy coming from faraway points like the sun and stars. They enter the point at the top of the pyramid. They then spread out as they travel downward, emanating through the wider base and continuing down into the earth.

This bi-directionality makes the pyramids so powerful. Add a second pyramid, downward pointing, and you get an octahedron. Now imagine this occurring naturally in octahedral crystal clusters. It occurs in several stone types, including Fluorite and Pyrite. These clusters and several free-standing varieties (such as Cuprite, Magnesite, Diamonds, and Spinel) are trying to form perfect octahedrons by melding the upward-facing pyramid with a downward-facing pyramid. An octahedron mirrors or doubles the effect of the initial, more basic single pyramid.

I consider octahedrons to be the religious symbol of the mineral world. It's just like the Star of David or the cross, in terms of representing the union of opposites: vertical/horizontal, up/down, heaven/earth. The fact that you can't be sure if the up pyramid is pulling down or sending up is reminiscent of the yin and yang symbol, which represents the Ancient Chinese philosophical concept of duality. Each half integrates pieces of the opposing half to create a balanced whole.

IMAGE 57 HEALING

ANGEL WING ANHYDRITE crystal (Mexico), more on page 141

An Angel's Touch

The whole concept of "as above, so below" is perfectly represented in this shape, making it also a visual representation of the relationship and interaction between our daily reality and the Dreamtime, or collective subconscious.

Octahedrons are often cut and polished out of Fluorite, which also cleaves naturally into octahedrons if the massive source material is molecularly configured to favor that. Anyhow, I like to keep octahedrons and octahedral clusters around as auspicious witnesses of (and participants in) my life.

IMAGE 38 octahedral cluster of **Pyrite** from Peru page 42

IMAGE 39 **Golden Scheelite** most often forms into octahedrons page 43

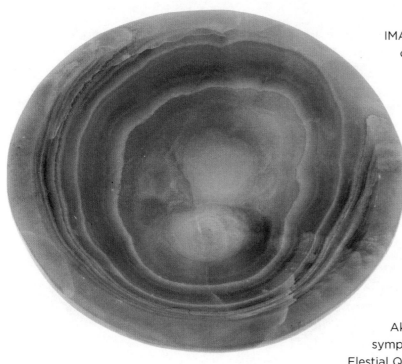

HEALING   IMAGE 58

BROWN ARAGONITE bowl (Argentina), more on page 141

Healing from Inside

13. Cathedral Quartz

Some Quartzes have a cascade of attached, but semi-separate crystals with trigonic terminations all down their sides. Some confuse these with record keepers, which they are not. It might be easy to imagine these housing Akashic Records because of their majestic symphony of triangles. For me, they're akin to Elestial Quartz and represent both age and wisdom. Additionally, like the cathedrals built in the Middle Ages, they require and evoke the notion of intricately planned and executed collaborations.

14. Phantoms

You have to see these to grasp how wonderful they are. Phantoms happen mostly in Quartz. They are an occurrence whereby differently colored sediments or a layer of, say, Smoky Quartz forms between other clear layers as the crystal grows in size over time. You end up seeing these little tent-remnants of earlier growth layers inside the larger crystal. These are often polished on the outside, so you can see inside more easily.

A lot has been written elsewhere (by other people) about the metaphorical significance of phantoms. The most obvious relevance for me is that they represent earlier stages of your development, as some fossils and Foundation stones do also. Since it's in a single crystal, I think of it more as a representation of your own individual history and process, rather than a collective thing. As such, I consider phantoms to be Self stones rather than Foundation stones.

Why is Chevron Amethyst not also considered a phantom? Because the layers are not translucent. What is an angel phantom? It's when instead of just being a coating, there seems to be a whole inner crystal of a different color, not clear but gauzy, and also not super defined in terms of its surface.

IMAGE 78 **Lithium Quartz** with a solid angel phantom crystal within page 84

IMAGE 161 eight-phantom **Smoky "green" Citrine** page 169

15. Growth Interference

Several varieties of Quartz look distinctly odd because they have formed in atypical ways. Quartz usually has six sides and a clearly defined six-sided point, tip, or termination. While some Growth Interference Quartz may have six distinct sides, the termination is anything but conventional and is often irregular, as in the case of etched crystals or Nirvana Quartz.

Energetically, Growth Interference crystals will not be your go-to for energy transmission. Growth Interference crystals are generally collectors' oddities. In the case of a Nirvana Quartz, however, the unusual formation is actually the source of its power.

IMAGE 125 **Nirvana Quartz**, African page 132

IMAGE 157 **Nirvana Quartz**, Himalayan page 165

IMAGE 162 classic **Growth Interference Quartz** page 171

IMAGE 164 etched **Ametrine** page 173

16. Manifestation (Child Within) Quartz

In this unusual occurrence of Quartz, and I've only ever seen it otherwise in Selenite. You have a smaller crystal entirely (or at least the point) enclosed within a larger crystal. It's like a fish in

IMAGE 59 HEALING

BLUE LACE AGATE heart-shaped geode (Namibia), more on page 142

Soothing the Layers

CACTUS QUARTZ AMETHYST unusually
harmonious cluster (South Africa), more
on page 60 + 142

Directed Healing

an aquarium, but usually it originates outside the bigger crystal, so it's not literally floating (in its entirety) inside the other crystal. You'll see the base of the point originate on the surface of the larger crystal, and its point lodged within it.

I first heard about these as being called Penetration Quartz, which may be the most geologically recognized term. Then I heard of them—and I think I like this name best—as Child Within crystals. Finally, and most recently, I've seen them most often called Manifestation Quartz. I'm okay with that name, mostly because it gives us a common language for talking about it. But the energy it speaks to much more is the idea of there being a special being, a child within, that is embraced and protected by the larger parent, friend, or older self.

17. Botryoidal Termination

Some non-Quartz clusters do not terminate in spikes, but instead in a bubbly, organic, and flowing fashion. We have three examples featured here, they make quite wonderful display pieces. The termination itself is not necessarily the source of the stone's energy, but it does contain or frame it nicely. Not pictured, Fluorite can also be botryoidal.

IMAGE 19 botryoidal **Rhodochrosite** crystal/chunk page 23

IMAGE 82 botryoidal **Green Prehnite** generally from Mali page 88

IMAGE 163 botryoidal **Hematite**
from Morocco page 172

HONEY CALCITE aka Golden Healer (USA),
more on page 143

Healing Sunset

18. Etching

When chemicals eat away at the side of a formed crystal, or it has a particular type of growth interference, you will see a lot of abstract formations on the crystal's siding. This is called etching. Some people love it, believing it gives the stone added collector or metaphysical value, while others don't care for it. Nirvana Quartz often exhibits both growth interference *and* etching. Etching is also something that occurs with other stones too—Topaz and Aquamarine come to mind.

IMAGE 125 **Nirvana Quartz**, more growth interference than etching page 132

IMAGE 164 classic example of etching, on an Anahi Mine **Ametrine** page 173

GEOMETRIC SHAPES

What is the difference between my categorization of geometric shapes (below) versus the types of crystallization outlined above? The geometric shapes are carved by people because they appreciate these forms and believe they have significance, independent of what you would find crystalizing naturally.

1. Merkaba

The Merkaba is a Kabbalistic variation of the octahedron. It is the merging of one three-sided pyramid—also called a tetrahedron—with another. One is pointing up and the other is pointing down. It's still got the superimposition of opposites going on, but takes it to a different level than the octahedron. Interestingly, although a seemingly simpler shape, it has eight points instead of six and has the disadvantage of not occurring in nature. Since I have the octahedron to work with already, I tend not to bother with the Merkaba. It is nonetheless a popular shape in the metaphysical community.

IMAGE 165 **Auralite** Merkaba page 174

2. Pyramids

In the octahedron section above, I explore one level of meaning regarding the pyramid. Since they are iconic, people appreciate having stones cut into this distinctive shape. It's a very stable structure that can condition a space, depending on its size. In other words, depending on the type of stone it's made of, a pyramid can project that energy out into the area surrounding it. It's less obtrusive than an obelisk or generator and feels like a better balance between masculine and feminine energies. In other words, the vertical to horizontal dimensions are in greater harmony or balance than you'll find in those other shapes.

HEALING   IMAGE 62

MILKY CALCITE cluster (Mexico), more on page 60 + 143

Nourishing Towards Health

3. Bowl

Although bowls are mostly functional, in terms of holding liquids, crystals, and other valuables, their shape is a lot like a radar scoop to the sky—a half globe, ready to receive. I often leave them wide open, particularly with nice materials like the ones featured here; a swipe of the fingers through it is like scooping up a moisturizer. It's rejuvenating and another good technique for synthesizing crystal energy.

IMAGE 58 **Brown Aragonite** bowl page 64

IMAGE 166 **Blue Calcite** bowl page 175

4. Sphere

I have never attempted to read clear crystal balls, but I can understand why it might be easy, if you were inclined to. It's a perfect shape for divination. Divination is generally thought to be a look into the future exclusively, but I consider it more of a look into the unknown, which might include elements of the past and present as well. What spheres have, which makes them uniquely qualified for this, is the fact that they're omnidirectional. That means they can pull to their center from all directions and can project energetically into all directions. This makes them continuously connected to everything, which I think is a prerequisite if you are trying to access other dimensions.

Why don't I use Quartz crystal balls for this purpose? Because I'm not actually interested in predicting the future or peering into the unknown, per se. While I once was able to identify some people's past lives, being a psychic is not on my own personal path. The two relevant areas that most interest me are the ethers of Spirit Community and the depths of the subconscious, for which I have other particular stone types to help me (from the Vision and Source energy zones).

For me, the shape of the sphere is most useful as a centerpiece in a layout or constellation. I've used a large green Fluorite sphere for this purpose. They are also great as palm pieces. I have a Lapis ball I've used like this, and an even larger Jade sphere comes to mind. Palm pieces facilitate the synthesizing of each stone's energy through our skin and nerve endings. I think spheres can also help focus and enhance Quartz clusters by sitting just so on their omnidirectional points.

IMAGE 6 **Dinosaur Gembone** sphere page 10

IMAGE 27 **Orange Calcite** sphere page 31

IMAGE 52 **Rose Quartz** sphere page 58

IMAGE 104 **Blue Apatite** sphere page 111

IMAGE 106 **Ocean Jasper** sphere page 113

IMAGE 145 **Golden Sheen Obsidian** sphere page 152

IMAGE 147 **Shungite** sphere with Pyrite inclusions page 154

IMAGE 63   HEALING

CANDLE QUARTZ 3-pointed relationship stone (South Africa), more on page 143

Compassionate Healing

5. Egg

The egg resembles a sphere if you look up at it from the bottom (the round side), which gives it the same general sense of omni-directionality as a sphere. What makes eggs different is that they are emergent—the top is like a sphere that grew and elongated, stretching taller. This is where the birth or new beginning energy comes from, and what makes an egg so special. It also fits into the hand easily, making for an excellent palm or meditation stone.

Eggs are cut out of every material you can imagine but are strangely not as popular as I think they deserve to be. I think people used to collect and display them on stands before so many other shapes came onto the market. Although they look great, I prefer using them in hand. Lavender Fluorite is almost exclusively cut into eggs, which I find to be a wonderful nerve tonic for when people need to relax, as they do at the start of a private session or meditation. Angelite eggs are sometimes left unpolished or matte in finish, which, along with Jade, feels particularly wonderful to the touch.

IMAGE 72 **Lavender Fluorite** egg page 78

IMAGE 90 **Chrysocolla** egg page 96

6. Palm Pieces

The classic palm piece is a perfect oval that fits comfortably in your hand with your fingers folded completely over it. However, any stone—chunk or crystal—that fits into your palm in the same way, could easily be called a palm piece too. Fortunately, these are made from many stones, but they're oddly not as available as I'd like (so I specialize in them).

We have a large number of sensitive nerve endings in our hands, as mentioned above. This size gives you maximum skin contact, which enables optimum synthesis of a stone's energy. If you're not using naturally formed crystals and are okay with using cut and polished material, the palm piece is an essential tool. You can also use them harmonically (same with the forms listed above and below), holding one type and energy in one hand and another type of energy in the other. This way, you

HEALING · · · · · · · · · · · · · · · · · · IMAGE 64

BLUE CELESTITE cluster (Madagascar), more on page 144

Gratitude, Heavenly Gifts and Mercies

can benefit from both. For example, one stone can do the grounding (Hematite) while the other connects us to our spirit community (green Fluorite). You can get the best of both worlds, so long as one is balancing, not overpowering the other. Often, though, depending on how the meditator is feeling, who they are and where they're at in their life, one does end up speaking more loudly to them than the other.

IMAGE 25 **Green Opal** palm piece page 29

IMAGE 86 **Snowy Carnelian** palm piece page 92

IMAGE 107 **Labradorite** palm piece page 114

IMAGE 108 **Ethiopian Opal** floater palm piece page 115

IMAGE 167 **Rose Quartz** palm piece page 176

7. Cylinders

Also known as Meditation Chargers or Harmonizers, cylinders are enjoying a bit of a vogue currently. In the Crystal World, when a new shape is discovered, it gets exploited to the max. This particular trend is not without merit. While palm pieces may be completely enclosed in the hand, cylinders go beyond our grip with flat-round ends extending out on either side of our closed fists. This allows for a continuous and independent energy flow for the stone to connect out into, and back from the world. Another convention that's come with this shape is the option to alternate stones, so you have one of each type in each hand acting together in a harmonic capacity, as I've suggested above with palm pieces. Cylinders can double as room conditioners too, if you leave them standing up like an obelisk or generator.

IMAGE 168 **Charoite** cylinder page 179

IMAGE 65   HEALING

INDIGO CHALCEDONY disc palm piece (unknown origin), more on page 144

Setting the Healing Standard

8. Worry Stones

Worry stones are small round or more often oval palm pieces, typically around 2" long, that have an indented "bowl" in the middle, running the length of the stone. These are for you to rub with your thumb, it's a kind

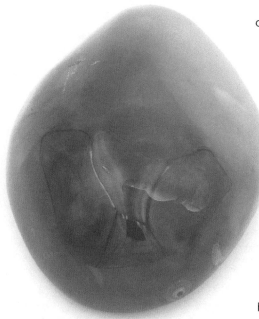

LAVENDER CHALCEDONY (Turkey), more on page 145
Restored Alignment

of stress-reducer. I've made them into pendants and people appreciate the fact that you can interact with them additionally in this way, rather than simply possessing or holding them. Again, your experience will vary based on what type of stone you get in this shape.

9. Tumbles, Pebbles

Tumbled stones are perhaps the lowest common denominator, the dollar bill or penny of the Crystal World, but they're oh-so handy. Generally cheap, they make it possible to collect a number of varieties without a huge outlay. I personally prefer larger stones for my purposes, but many people swear by the tumblers and for some people, that can be enough. They're great for grids or constellations, if you need a lot of one type of stone. You can have all chakras represented handily in a pouch. They'll fit into your pocket (or pocketbook) with ease. And most can play well together, in the sense that they can knock against one another without breaking. Energetically, some people worry about mixing the wrong stones together—like medications that are contraindicated—but I think with stones, particularly small ones like this, they tend to get on pretty well with one another.

10. Spacers, or Equilibrium Stones

I mention these later in the book, but wanted to highlight them here, among the types of shapes that are useful for oneself and when working with others. In this case what you use is not as important as the fact that it does not have or carry its own agenda, except simply to mark, maintain, and enhance sacred safe space. Multiple, uniformly shaped items, tumblers, or sticks can do this job perfectly. Set them generally in a circular way, around yourself, a layout of stones, or a person who's getting a treatment.

11. Pendulums

Many of my customers swear by pendulums. I have no idea how, but they and dowsing rods have been used to find lost objects and locate water sources. Mostly, I've seen them used for all manner of decision-making, including for buying crystals. There's so much lore out there that I won't attempt to duplicate any of it, except to say that pendulums are popular. I have seen a pendulum swung in front of a medium's face to tease out information and enhance communication with the spirits around her clients. I personally would use them to hold over an affected area, if I wanted to pinpoint and deliver a particular energy dose to that site.

12. Generator

Generators point straight up, are generally squat, and can be large or small. Think milk carton shapes. Size will indicate how much surrounding space they can condition. I've mentioned the word condition a few times and want to make sure I'm clear about what that means. To condition a room means to set the tone or otherwise impact it. So, for example, a Milky Quartz would bring the energy of compassion to a room, or if super clear, clarity would be its contribution to the space. Red Jasper would bring stability, and so forth.

IMAGE 132 natural **Apophyllite** generator point page 139

IMAGE 135 **Blue Tara Quartz** generator page 142

IMAGE 146 natural **Lemurian** generator page 153

IMAGE 169 **Blue Quartz** generator page 178

13. Obelisk

To imagine an obelisk, think of perhaps the best known one, the Washington Monument (modeled, actually, after ancient Egyptian obelisks). Obelisks can be used as wands, but they have a flattened four-sided base so they can stand primarily. They project energy upwards more than outwards or around themselves. I think of an obelisk more at the gateway of a room or to denote sacred space on the sides, and a

IMAGE 67   HEALING

PINK CHALCEDONY PETRIFIED WOOD (USA), more on page 145

Personal Care

generator as something you would more likely see in the center of the room (or altar). Unless, as the Egyptians originally imagined it, you want to use it to honor someone or some deity. In that case, it can assume more of a central placement.

IMAGE 112 **Astrophyllite** obelisk page 119

IMAGE 170 **Ametrine** obelisk page 179

14. Wands

Wands are for harnessing, focusing, and transmitting energies or intentions of your choice. Although they feature prominently in children's books and Harry Potter, they are anything but child's play. I'd like to see more people turning to wands in their practise. They can be as simple as an obelisk, elongated carved/polished, or a natural point. And they can get more complex, with a sphere at one end (receiver), central rod (or conveyer), and dedicated point (transmitter). Some have feathers attached. I've carried ones that have long Selenite rods or blades for rituals like spreading sage, or cutting cords (which release things that no longer serve us).

Wands can be used like a hand-held transmitter, pointing or pulling from any direction of your choice. Notice I used the word pulling. That's because you (or the piece sometimes automatically) can reverse polarity, and instead of sending energy as you would predict through its point, it pulls back energy right through the point of the wand itself (and into you).

IMAGE 140 **Larvikite** polished and rounded massage wand page 147

IMAGE 171 **Lemurian** natural laser wands page 128 + 180

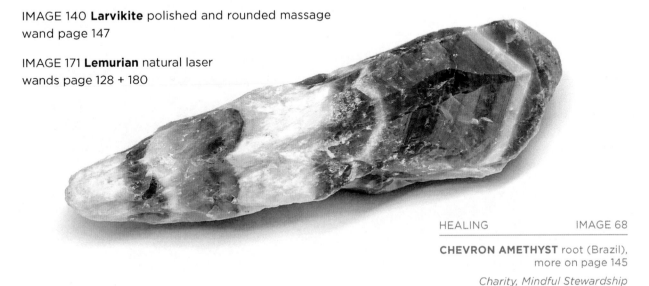

HEALING   IMAGE 68

CHEVRON AMETHYST root (Brazil),
more on page 145

Charity, Mindful Stewardship

15. Heart

I like the universal appeal of the heart symbol. It refers to love, and who can find fault with that? Some people might find it cheesy, but I've come to embrace them. They provide very quick access to a concept most people can relate to. What makes each one different is the size, shape, and the material it's made of. For example, a Pyrite heart would be grounding and also appealing to our need for boundaries and interpersonal balance. A Fluorite heart could symbolize a spiritual bond. You can see images of the four hearts pictured in this book below.

IMAGE 46 pair of connected **Lepidolite** hearts page 52

IMAGE 53 **Smoky Quartz** heart page 59

IMAGE 117 pair of connected **Aquamarine Fluorite** hearts page 124

IMAGE 172 large gemmy Peruvian **Rhodochrosite** heart page 182

IMAGE 69   HEALING

CINTAMANI STONE layered Obsidian (Indonesia), more on page 146

Ancient Healing

What I hope you're seeing as we survey all these crystal forms is that what we do with crystals can often be determined or enhanced by what physical shape they're in. The form itself—and the stone it's made of—does a lot of the work. We just select and position, choosing the type of intention and energies we want to harness.

SCULPTURAL REPRESENTATIONS

Sculptural Representations of the type we'll be discussing below are not necessarily Entity Stones, a particular variety I talk about in Section Three. The reason is that these don't necessarily house or embody the beings they represent. Often the likeness is simply that, a likeness. Mass produced items

can be lovely but unconvincing, or at least not emotionally moving in terms of how they portray a certain deity or skull, for example. Particularly expert sculptors are able to imbue their pieces with such personality that they suddenly take on more of the identity of that which they were trying to represent, capturing, for example, the true essence of a lion (or other being) in the carving. As with all the other forms we've been discussing, the type of stone is relevant. So, for example, a Lapis Buddha may confer more wisdom in communication, while a Jade Buddha is more reassuring (see such a Buddha on page 188).

1. Angels

Generally, angels are carved without too much detail, but they do exist in a surprising range of stones and design styles. I like carrying them at my shop and seeking them out because I appreciate them. I don't follow or invoke specifically named angels, but I do consider angels among the pantheon of benevolent spirit guides and companions available to us, so I'm not at odds with those who do.

IMAGE 173 **Yellow Fluorite** angel page 184

HEALING   IMAGE 70

COBALTO CALCITE rounded cluster (Morocco), more on page 147
Physical Heart Healing

2. Animals

If you like horses, cats, and dogs—or wild animals—this is a wonderful option. A carving of one of your favorite animals is nice to have around to remind you of it, and what it may represent for you. If you have a totemic or spirit animal, this can be particularly useful too, as it becomes the focus of your journeying and a connection point for the evolution of your shamanic self. It might help you to have a watchdog carving as a tangible representation of protection on your altar (or in the corners of your house). Perhaps a bird carving might help you imagine sending messages afar. I've chosen to picture a fanciful dragon in this book, but the possibilities are limitless here.

IMAGE 174 **Sugilite** dragon page 186

3. Deities

The carving of deities into stone dates back tens of thousands of years. One of my favorites is the Venus of Willendorf, which goes back 30,000 years (making it three times as old as the advent of agriculture). Later, people began to carve Ganesh, Buddha, Jesus, Qwan Yin, and the list goes on. They still do, and it's all good, particularly if you're an adherent to the belief systems they represent. A lot of people who don't even follow Buddhism like to have a Buddha around. I know I've purchased a number for my shop, and people really appreciate them.

IMAGE 175 **Nephrite Jade** Buddha page 188

IMAGE 71 HEALING

PINK DANBURITE large cluster (Mexico), more on page 60 + 147

Receiving Higher Love

4. Skulls

I often get the question, "Why skulls? What is it about them that people like?" Certainly, the internet is awash with crystal skull lore, but I don't follow any of that. I used to be spooked by them, now I really like them. Here's why.

First of all, skulls represent a part of our anatomy that lives on and with more personality than other bones in our body. Secondly, they represent what's left after we go, our own personal legacy—what people will remember us by. And last but not least, stone skulls can help us feel connected with our loved ones who've passed over to the other side. Once I came up with these three explanations, I found it easy to advocate for these mysterious and misunderstood representations of the human being.

IMAGE 176 **Bumblebee Jasper** skull page 190

HEALING   IMAGE 72

LAVENDER FLUORITE egg (China),
more on page 147
Calming the Nerves

Crystal Placements

IN HAND

This is one of my favorite ways to experience crystals and where I developed a preference for larger, at least palm sized pieces. Recently, I've also begun to appreciate spheres and eggs for this same purpose. When you hold a crystal like this in your hand, you're engaging touch, sight, and the imagination with a total focus on the piece's energy signature (relative to just putting it into your bag or on a table). I find that if you've paused to hold a crystal—rather than just having it around—you're more likely to be focused on its meaning, less distracted, and more able to create a healing relationship with it (and yourself).

POCKET/PURSE

If there are some stones you like and you want to have them around—but you're not going to have time to pause and be with them—tossing them (respectfully) into your bag, backpack, or pocket's a great way to bring 'em along for the ride and give yourself an extra boost of their energies. Plus, it's there if you want it while you're waiting in line or have some down time—you can take them out and contemplate with them for an ad hoc meditation.

JEWELRY

Although a great deal smaller—with the exception of larger pendants—jewelry is a great way to commune and travel with your favorite stones in a very personal way. You don't even need a bag, purse, or pocket, 'cause it's on you the whole time. I wear a Jade ring, through which I imagine all my blood passes and that's kind of cool to consider. It's like a conditioner for our circulatory system.

I like pendants particularly, to set the tone for the day—maybe Jade for a family day or Sugilite for a day (among many) that I want to really focus on manifesting. Lately, I've been addicted to wearing Moldavite. Sometimes I wear nothing for a break. In my business, I have focused mostly on pendants because they're so versatile—sizing is not an issue (as it is with rings)—and you can swap out chains easily.

Necklaces can be uniquely wonderful. I'll wear Butterscotch Amber if I'm in the process of healing, Rhodochrosite if I want to be fully present in my vitality, or Smoky Quartz to mellow me out and prevent any stress or bad will before it gets a hold of me. When I say necklaces, I mean the whole thing around your neck is made up of stones. It's a bit more heavy handed (energetically) than a pendant, but sometimes that's what is called for. I have a sweet mix of Quartz and Rudraksha beads in a necklace— they're not stone—but as a dried seed, they speak to our potential, new beginnings, and steppling light.

Bracelets are great too, if they don't interfere with your typing on a computer, which they tend to (for me). They're like a glorified ring. My wife wears a Jade bangle permanently (on her wrist), but you have to get the right size for it to be always comfortable. And we've learned the hard way that

IMAGE 73   HEALING

PINK FLUORITE octahedral cluster (Mexico), more on page 60 + 148

Spiritual Heart Healing

HERKIMER DIAMOND QUARTZ tabular crystal (NY, USA), more on page 149

The Fortress, Health & Strength

the best method for putting them on is with a plastic bag over your hand, so you can get a tight fit on and off easily. A woman at a show refused our offer of the bag and sent the bangle flying (and shattering) onto the concrete floor. You break it, you pay for it.

IMAGE 38 **Hypersthene pendant** page 38

IMAGE 40 **Super Seven pendant** page 44

IMAGE 80 **Midnight Lace Obsidian pendant** page 86

IMAGE 177 (40+ gram) **Moldavite pendant** with Sterling chain page 198

Bedside

It's very important to note that the same crystal may affect you differently in the day than it might in the night. You have to be mindful of your dreams in case a stone is stirring up things you'd rather not experience while you're trying to rest. In the case that it's trouble, don't hesitate to remove it from your bedside.

Someone recently asked about putting a certain stone they'd bought under their pillow. "It's too small" I warned. I was afraid it would get lost and later vacuumed up inadvertently. My wife banned me from putting stones in the bed 'cause she once hit her head on one. Having them on shelves, in your night table, or even under the bed (where I keep a big ol' river worn Jade) is a whole lot safer.

Having stones in your bedroom is a bit like taking them out during your day. Only this time you're bringing them along for the ride at night. Given that we spend roughly one third of our lives sleeping, this is a pretty significant opportunity for you to interface with crystals energetically (albeit while you're snoozing).

There's also all the time you're not there, not in your bedroom, to consider. During your time away, the stones you have in your bedroom (and at your home in general) sort of hold down the fort, keep the fire burning, and set the tone for the sacred space that you can look forward to returning to.

Altar

Nowhere is the arrangement and content of your collection more relevant than in a place you've consecrated as sacred, where you revisit all your hopes and dreams through devoted meditation and attention.

I don't have an altar per se. I suppose one could argue that my store and its meditation rooms serve as my altars. My bedside table is a bit of an altar, given all the crystals and jewelry I have in it.

While what you have on your altar is not as portable as some of the other suggestions I've made, it makes up in gravity what it lacks in mobility. It's almost like—and probably often is—a constellation, layout, or permanent grid. It is there that your favorite pieces and all they represent reside and do their good work on your life.

IMAGE 75   HEALING

JET chunk (Poland), more on page 150

Internal Clearing

At your Desk / At Work

What works about having your favorite stones on your desk (so long as it doesn't get cluttered energetically) is that you can contemplate them during or between calls, even pick them up and take a short meditation break with them. This is different from traveling with them or having them in other parts of your home. For starters if they're public, people can see them, comment on them. This may work on your video conferencing calls, if they're not distracting. In a physical workplace, people might not be able to help themselves from fondling your rocks when you're not looking, which might make you feel vulnerable. In that case, hide them or bring them out only when you're there.

On the upside, it can be nice and even necessary to have stones in your workspace, particularly if you're looking to protect against unpleasant vibes from your co-workers or the work environment in general. Stones like Smoky Quartz or Shungite and Black Tourmaline can help defend against electromagnetic frequencies. Clear Quartz, lasers, wands, and obelisks can help with your concentration.

At Home in Your Space

If you're self-employed, receiving people in a larger work space, or even just upleveling the vibration of your home, there is much written out there about what you should do: stones in the four corners, by the doors, etcetera. I have not exercised these options myself. I feel like the many other recommendations

I've made in this section suffice, but I'm certainly not opposed to you going that extra mile, but only if you feel it will make that much of a difference.

One thing I do suggest, if you're in the healing or consulting/counseling trades, is to have crystals under your treatment table or on the coffee table between you and your clients. I prefer larger Quartz and Amethyst clusters or Selenite for this purpose. These can set the tone for every session, and help you observe proper boundaries during your interactions.

On the Body

Different from jewelry, we're talking here about the laying of loose stones onto your body. You may have seen it in crystal books, photos of a body lying supine, with 30 stones on it. That feels like too many competing energies to me. I share the motivation to impact the body favorably with a set of stones, but far fewer will do the job more effectively. Otherwise, it becomes energetically overwhelming for the recipient and everyone loses focus as to the purpose of the process.

Remember, you can also do this on your own. I know a woman who lies down and places a single stone on the center of any given chakra. She does this as a focal point for meditation and to harness the energy of that stone and its chakra.

When I do sessions with people, we use a succession of paired stones held in the hands. As we move on, they get laid on the ground next to them (or occasionally left on their person for a while). The stones communicate through the body what I'm saying (in terms of our guided experience), traveling through the hands, eyes, ears and other surfaces. Sometimes, for the stones to communicate directly to certain parts of the body, placing them there makes the most sense (on the belly or chest for example).

HEALING   IMAGE 76

LARIMAR (Dominican Republic), more on page 150
Healing through the Waters

Third Eye Stones

Third eye stones have to fit just so on the forehead (and ideally not fall off). Generally, they should be around an inch or smaller, even better if they have a little curvature, and can nestle on your forehead, over your brow, or just above the bridge of your nose. I have occasionally led groups in this kind of meditation, and when I do, it's always super powerful. You can put a grounding stone on the forehead and feel grounding there in a way that's totally unique (and not the way we normally experience it).

Ascension stones seem to work even more rapidly than usual when placed over the third eye. And best of all, tiny pieces that would otherwise be passed over, can come into play quite effectively. This is a very rich area to explore, one you should definitely try out on your own. When I do it in a group, everyone's heads are either pointing in, and at the center. Or everyone's feet can be in the center, maybe pressing against a large center stone, and their bodies and heads emanate outward in a radial pattern.

Working with Crystals

This phrase is quite important to grasp and comprehend. It's about our connection and collaboration with crystals for a purpose. From the subtitle of this book, our primary goal is to understand and specifically to work with stones for clarity and flow.

Financially, I could probably have done better for myself by simply focusing on the selling of crystals, disregarding the metaphysically educational piece. A lot of people do, and that's quite enough for them. Many use the trappings of crystal healing as a sales pitch.

IMAGE 77 HEALING

LINGAM STONE (India), more on page 151
Equilibrium Stone

Working with crystals is the whole point of my entire career. It would be meaningless for me if I didn't have a core interest in teaching people to bring stones into their lives more meaningfully. It takes a lot of time on my part—planning and preparing—and in terms of promoting and delivering my meditations, classes, and community offerings. Even

writing this book has been a huge undertaking, but all so worth it, because it forces me to comb through my teachings and make more sense of them for you. It's a responsibility really, to you and to the force of inspiration that launched me on this journey. It is the culmination for me, of what it means to work with crystals. Whether you buy from me or work with me is not so important as that I've done my best to lay bare my knowledge and understanding.

For many, the journey is not so deep. A lot of us are stuck on the aesthetics of stones. The majority of buyers operate at this level and that suits them fine. Indeed, the majority of crystal sales are made off looks alone. Glitter sells.

But if you're reading this book, I'm sure you hunger for more yourself. Others may consider crystals a spectator sport. You and I are teaming up to experience crystals as the participatory sport I think they are meant to be. It takes our involvement and commitment to get the full value out of our experience with crystals. This is ultimately what I mean by working with crystals.

HEALING   IMAGE 78

LITHIUM QUARTZ point (Brazil), more on page 151
Mental Healing

FEELING CRYSTAL ENERGY

Geo-sentience, the word I've created to describe the capacity some of us have to sense crystals, is an important building block of your experience with stones. I didn't have it until I suddenly did, through no effort of my own. You might be like that, or you might be totally insensitive to the energy of stones. What I find is that those who are still drawn to stones, or simply hang out with a friend who's into them, some-times chance upon a major breakthrough that opens the flood gates to their own geo-sentience. That's what happened to me!

Here's another example. A couple of women who came into my shop—one had never felt anything from a stone. As her friend walked around and found the things she was looking for, we somehow touched on the subject of purple Jade. I fetched a few pieces for her and when she held one, she suddenly started to tear up. It had struck a chord and opened her heart. She bought the piece on the spot and commissioned me to have it wrapped into a pendant for her.

Not all breakthroughs are so explicit, but I do encourage you to check out lots of stones, pick them up, feel them. Follow your interests, or those of your friends and family. While many may leave you cold, be open to the possibility that eventually one will open up to you. It does happen. And when it does, you'll want to use that opening to widen your sensitivity, becoming increasingly open to the energy of other stones.

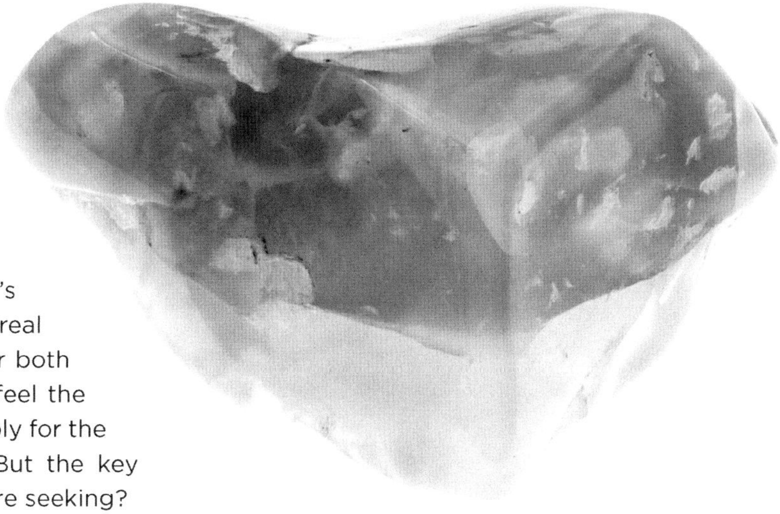

CRYSTAL HEALING

Crystal Healing is generally the holy grail of people's interest in crystals. It's a phrase that's thrown around too freely, I think, but it's a real thing. Of course it's more effective if one or both parties (healer and recipient) can actually feel the crystal energies. Sometimes it's enough simply for the practitioner to know what they're doing. But the key question is, what is the goal or outcome we're seeking?

IMAGE 79   HEALING

MOON QUARTZ tumbler (AZ, USA), more on page 152

Healing our Vision

We've already established in Part One that promising quick panaceas and easy prescriptions is not where we're at. If it works for you to keep it that simple, go for it. One problem, one stone solution, presto! However, I prefer a more nuanced approach. It's not entirely dissimilar though, it's just more sophisticated and goes a little something like this.

Someone's stressed out and anxious, find them calming and soothing stones. Someone's afraid, create a safe space and a respite from the storm. Someone's in pain, no promises, but I've seen people transcend their pain through journeying in meditation. Family of origin issues, work with Foundation stones. Feeling in a rut, Vision stones come in handy. The list goes on.

Total cure is not the goal, or even necessarily possible. Sometimes the tsunami of an illness is too great to mitigate. Amelioration in the moment, allowing and welcoming your own natural healing tendencies, this can create lasting value. Wellness is a relative term, I'd prefer crystal wellness to crystal healing as a term for what we do. It's more universally applicable and doesn't create false expectations.

And remember, you are not alone as a client or a practitioner. There are other modalities and modern science that can work their own wonders on your behalf. You have to think of healing as teamwork, a collaboration. Ideally, it takes a village to heal each person. Holistic is not just an internal goal, it should be a community value and undertaking.

Crystals can have an important role to play in the process. As our book title suggests, we want to use them for clarity and flow. That means pursuing the inquiry—discovering and getting clear on what's really going on inside, what are you needing and hoping for at this moment. Once that becomes clear, and the proper tools are brought into play, it becomes easier to facilitate flow. You want your energy and that of the universe to become more synchronized, without blockage or bottlenecks, so life energy can travel through you untethered. The goal is for you to achieve a sense of maximum personal wellness and satisfaction.

THE POWER OF IMAGINATION

A key determinant as to whether you can be helped (or make something happen) with crystals in your life stems from your capacity to imagine. The mind itself is perhaps our most powerful healing tool—the psychological sciences are increasingly recognizing this—and if you come up empty on feeling energies and journeying, it can become that much harder to make things move for you, metaphysically.

Imagination is like a muscle, it's a strength that can be developed. Cultivating it can be a goal in itself. That's why people take psychic development classes, to find and build on capabilities they might not have been born with or that they haven't developed previously. Think art classes, ballroom dance, anything that you don't start with automatic mastery over, but could become proficient in with some learning and effort.

I recommend that you flex your imagination muscles. Since we've already established that we are not dealing with the tangible, quantifiable world, it's essential. The five senses (or any subset of them) are all great. But if you have any hope of accessing or interfacing with the intangible world, you must develop your sixth sense.

Honesty really helps as well. Some people don't want to look at what's really going on inside. They claim to want healing, but sometimes an illness or limiting worldview is strangely self-serving. Perhaps it's somehow safer being a victim, you can take less responsibility that way. You can also become your own worst enemy this way, and could be the one standing in the way of your own progress.

I have found that people who refuse traditional talk therapy are also at a disadvantage because they are not allowing an objective

HEALING   IMAGE 80

MIDNIGHT LACE OBSIDIAN pendant (Mexico), more on page 152

Healing through the Layers

third party to have a say in their world. The universe is a great big objective third party, even though we experience it subjectively. To work with metaphysical forces, you have to open yourself up to the louder voice of a more universal reality and the supernatural (both of which operate largely outside of our own limited sphere of perception and control).

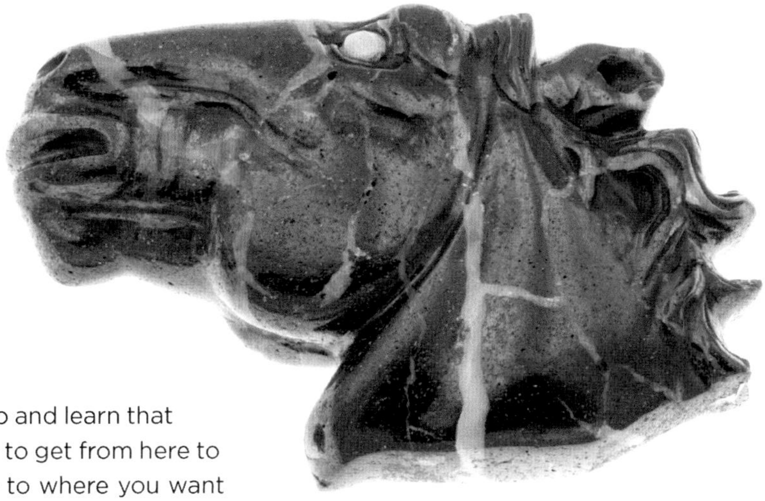

There are exercises and practices you can do and learn that will help you in this area. Think bridges, how to get from here to there. How do you get from where you are to where you want to be? You have to be willing to let go of preconceived notions and to explore new angles (and dimensions) if you want to get to the other side of any particular challenge, undertaking, or situation.

IMAGE 81   HEALING

BOULDER OPAL horse carving (Australia), more on page 153

Holding Fast

When we are sick or unhappy, we've reached a possible dead end that we have to somehow reverse out of. When that happens, it's the universe telling us it's time to try something new, something different. And it's always a test of our imagination to find that other way, think outside of the box, and get ourselves to a better place.

CRYSTAL MEDITATION

More than any other single activity, I've found that meditation is my key entry point for working with crystals. I offer in-person and online meditations, and while I don't teach classes on developing your capacity for imagination or finding your geo-sentience, this is as close as I get to that offering. I'm confident that if you follow this practice, solo or in groups, it will move you much further along on your spiritual path with crystals. Let me show you how it's done.

First, you want to engage in what I call the bio-med portion of your meditation. In this case "med" refers to meditation, not medical, and "bio" refers to biological, i.e. your body. Dedicate some time to being in a quiet place, without interruptions. Personally, I prefer to sit cross-legged with my back upright, but I've gotten used to leading meditations from a chair as well. That tends to be easier when I'm presenting online. You can lie down on the floor if you have someone else leading the meditation. Otherwise your body may confuse being supine with sleep, which deserves to be its own separate experience.

GREEN PREHNITE botryoidal cluster (Mali),
more on page 154

The Stone Aloe Vera

Next, close your eyes and turn your consciousness inward, leaving the demands and distractions of the social world behind. Focus on deepening your breath by inhaling for longer and allowing your exhalations to lengthen, expelling more of whatever needs to go from your lungs. Let your mind get quieter, allowing thoughts and sensations to pass through you, as if using a revolving door.

Scan your body, directing your awareness to your feet, legs, waist, torso, arms, and head. Reach out to your furthest extremities, inviting every cell to join the party, to be seen and appreciated for the important role they play in making you whole. I do this slightly differently and with varying imagery each time, as can you. I often include some grounding segment where you root into your body and extend that dynamic of reassuring connection to the chair, the bed, the floor, the building, the earth itself, and any extension of physical space you want to bring into play (the neighborhood, city, state, country, continent).

When I'm leading a meditation, particularly in person, we pause between segments. I punctuate with sound, using brass bells, a feather, or a frame drum, even a stone bracelet that I swish around in my hands to sound like a bubbling stream. You can use some of these instruments if you wish to clear the air, get a sense of completion, and set the stage for what's next. Attendees are invited to share what they've experienced, wherever it is that they're at or wanting to be, and you too can do that (if you're solo) to process and assimilate what you've experienced during each part of your meditation.

Then you prepare to receive stone energy—the intercession of an object that's been around thousands or even millions of years longer than you—with what I call the lightning rod principal. A lightning rod is a magnet for attracting lightning from the sky to connect and ground through a metal pole into the earth. It accommodates and focuses tremendous energy, successfully finding a home and direction for the bolt of electricity without causing any damage in the process. When you work with/hold a stone, together you

NAICA SELENITE crystal (Mexico), more on page 155
Clearly Sealing

become the lightning rod, suddenly connected to the universal in a way that was simply not possible when it was only you sitting there. That is the gravity and potential of meditating with a crystal.

What follows is the recipe or menu that you've created beforehand. I can lead meditations completely improvisationally, but I prefer to prepare when leading meditations myself, particularly so that my attendees don't have to. Plan out what you want to explore in this particular meditation. Do you want to make sure you have a grounding stone present? Are you wanting to connect with your spirit guides using ascension stones? Is there some part of your heart that needs healing? Maybe more than one of these things is true. I've done plenty of single stone meditations, but I have maxed out at about five stones in a single meditation because I don't think we can focus on more than that productively during one sitting. Also, you don't even have to have the stones themselves present, as I've learned from leading virtual meditations. Having a card or even the thought of a particular stone fleshed out can produce similar results.

The goal of a meditation, and indeed of a healing or wellness session, is to get from one place to another. It really is a journey, from a place of need to a place of feeling met and supported—ideally feeling better— moving along to a place where you feel more equipped to face the future.

DISTANCE HEALING

There are a few barriers I'd like to mention that I think can be crossed productively, particularly as you become more advanced in your work with crystals. One is time, reaching backward or forwards, and to those who've passed on. Another is reaching across great distances, to other parts of the globe. And the third is reaching over the consciousness divide to someone who is unable or unwilling to comprehend or consciously receive whatever it may be that you're trying to do for them. I won't get any more particular, as this would be better saved for a future book or training where I can give it the space it deserves, but I will recommend using Source and Channel stones, wands, and transmitters for these undertakings.

Crystals for Life

PROTECTION

Whether we have fantastic visions of what we want to undertake metaphysically—for which we need special protections—or whether we simply want to be safe in the world we live in daily, there are many stones that can help.

These are mostly Channel stones, which have to do with modulating the movement of energy through space, particularly by allowing or impeding it. You can sub-group these two at a time, because each pair has related functions as a duet.

HEALERITE SERPENTINE chunk (South Africa), more on page 155

Rebirthing

- ⬦ **Black Tourmaline** (Limits and Borders) — **CHANNEL**
- ⬦ **Black Tourmalinated Quartz** (Omnidirectional Boundaries) — **CHANNEL**
- ⬦ **Shungite** (Filtering Out the Negative) — **CHANNEL**
- ⬦ **Smoky Quartz** (Transmuting Toxicity) — **CHANNEL**
- ⬦ **Nuumite** (Cosmic Protection) — **CHANNEL**
- ⬦ **Larvikite** (Defensive Reflection), more close range — **CHANNEL**
- ⬦ **Morion Smoky Quartz** (The Guardian Stone) — **CHANNEL**
- ⬦ **Irradiated Smoky Quartz** (The Attack Dog) — **CHANNEL**
- ⬦ **Ventifact** (the Black Torch, Remover of Obstacles) — **CHANNEL**
- ⬦ **Jet** (Internal Clearing) — **HEALING**

Note that Jet is the only one from this list that's not a Channel stone. It's a Healing stone for when you want to cleanse yourself of some internal gunk or because you find that you have become your own worst enemy.

Black Tourmaline is kind of like the bumper of your car. Use it to mark territory, like a fence or wall. I also like to think of it like those giant metal, rubber, and cement buffers at train stations. At the end of the line, they're set up to keep the train from careening into the station in case the breaks don't work. Likewise, if someone is bad at honoring boundaries, this helps create a physical marker for keeping them at bay. Many people swear by Black Tourmaline to protect against EMFs and keep it by their computer (I prefer Smoky Quartz, which I explain later in this section).

In the case of Tourmalinated Quartz, that's ideal in an obelisk or sphere (something polished and standing). A customer of mine placed theirs in a central window to help set boundaries in numerous directions because their house was at the end of a T and they thought it was a good defense against problematic feng shui. Feng shui is also known as Chinese geomancy and it claims to harmonize individuals with their surrounding environment. Consider it also protective in multiple dimensions because the Tourmaline crystals do shoot off in so many directions.

Shungite sorts energy, keeping out the bad or non-supportive (even toxic), letting in the salutary. But toxicity gets around, and for when it's gotten into you (or past the barriers), Smoky Quartz is ideal. Smoky Quartz is colored the way it is due to its exposure to natural radioactivity in the ground. It transmutes negative energy, rendering it harmless, which is why it's not radioactive itself. For that reason, I find it to be the ultimate for EMF protection and wish I had a cell phone case made of it.

Nuumite and Larvikite are reflectors, they send back malintent to where it came from like a mirror. I like to reference the Kuba people's nail figurines from the Congo when talking about this dynamic. They hold a mirror over their belly for the same purpose and also take the nails for you, so you don't have to. In this case, these stones don't retain or absorb the negative energy, they dispel it. Larvikite protects locally—here on this plane—and the Nuumite does the same on a more cosmic level.

We have two stones that deal with threats from outside. The Morion Quartz acts as a guardian, looking over us and watching our back when we're not looking. It gives us rest and a sense of safety. Some Morions also double as Healing stones, similar to Jet, due to a certain type of color saturation and matte surface texture. To go on the offensive, or bark and attack, we have Irradiated Quartz. Consider

IMAGE 85   HEALING

SKELETAL aka **FENSTER QUARTZ** crystal (Mexico), more on page 155

Strength in spite of Weakness

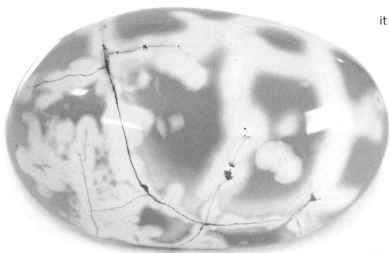

LIGHT SNOWY CARNELIAN palm piece
(Madagascar), more on page 156
Spiritual Resorbtion

it like a dog that not only defends its family (as would the Morion), but it has a chip on its shoulder, perhaps due to having been artificially irradiated, or like an over-disciplined animal (or person). Beware of friendly fire from Irradiated Quartz, it can turn on you if you point it toward yourself or a loved one.

Lastly, we have two additional stones that are protective in nature. The Basalt Ventifact (meaning wind-made in Latin), I call it the black torch. I've also dubbed it the remover of obstacles. Like the Indian deity Ganesh, it clears the way. This type of Ventifact (there are others, made of different materials) helps us to see ahead and advance in the darkness. I often recommend this when people are looking for movement in their lives. They're uncertain and need faith to step forward. The Ventifact offers that type of security, but only if you're headed in the right direction. It's a bit of a chicken and egg type of situation. You don't want to step off the cliff unless it's safe to do so, but if you really listen to the Ventifact, it won't lead you off a cliff. It leads you only to where you are predestined to go.

Jet offers a very different type of protection. It's actually an after-the-fact clean-up stone. It's ideal if you're seeking internal cleansing. It is pure within, as we should strive to be. Consider it like an internal shower. Gives you a fresh start.

HEALTH

Thinking about Illness

It's too bad that when we think of health, we think first of illness. If nothing's wrong, we don't give our health a second thought. We just go about our lives, taking our well-being entirely for granted.

Unfortunately, sickness can hit you in so many ways. Pain, loss of function, deep in the organs. It seems like we can be a bottomless pit of physical suffering. Just as we can be replete with joy and delight with life, so too can we be the opposite, which can leave us feeling depressed and hopeless.

Beyond our options for physical woe, we are equally prone to mental, emotional, and spiritual suffering. Loss and trauma wreak havoc on our being. Sometimes it feels like wellness is just an illusion, a cruel carrot, dangled perpetually out of reach.

There is a stone I find particularly helpful to consider for this part of the conversation. It's Skeletal or Fenster Quartz. Apart from Herkimer Diamonds (both hail from the Healing energy zone)—which represent the strong, complete, healthy, and defended being— Skeletal Quartzes are almost identical but have visible fractures within, symbolizing a weakness within a larger context of strength. The idea here is that we can have limitations and suffer illness in one part of our body or being, but there may be many other parts of ourselves that are in perfectly good shape—and that we can draw from or lean upon—for support in our time of need.

IMAGE 87   HEALING

DARK SNOWY CARNELIAN palm piece (Madagascar), more on page 156

Physical Resorption

IMAGE 85 **Skeletal Quartz** page 91

Each condition may call for different treatments, as would be true of any modality, or for any medical intervention. It's best to pull from wherever help may be available. You'll see the extremely ill open themselves up to experimental treatments, and people whose backs are against the wall turn to religion for solace, taking seriously again the matters of spirit that have now crowded in on them.

You must come to an understanding about what it is that is going on inside. What has gone wrong? Where do you want things to go from here? If you can't answer or visualize in these areas, your road will be harder and possibly longer. It's good to seek counsel, from whatever quarter you can find it, to help you answer these pressing questions.

Just as in the saying "an ounce of prevention is worth more than a pound of cure," what can you do now that will favorably affect your condition down the line? Asking yourself questions as I have posed above is an important part of the healing process.

I have often heard this phrase, like a ghostly voice in a chamber asking, "What do you think will happen?" I take it to mean, where do you think your current actions will take you? Or conversely, for healing, what is your endgame? What is the outcome you are specifically shooting for?

Approaching your situation with clarity of both inquiry and intention will go a long way towards advancing your cause.

I've had people approach me asking, "What crystal is good for the adrenal glands?" Or they'll ask about conditions so obscure that I haven't even heard of them. I don't want to make light of these occasions, but I have trouble hearing such questions. Let me explain why.

I'm no doctor. I hate to make stone prescriptions when there are perfectly adequate medications and treatments already out there. I'll always suggest people get standard medical care, assuming it's effective.

The unfortunate fact is that many people have gone the medical route and they're not getting the answers they need. You'll want to separate what are fair questions for the doctors, and what might be more appropriate to discuss with a therapist. And there are spiritual issues neither may be able to help you with. These are more in the court of the clergy or metaphysicians.

HEALING   IMAGE 88

WATER QUARTZ tumbler (Brazil), more on page 157

Wash it Away

No one likes taking medication if they don't have to. Side effects can be terrible. Healing naturally is always preferable. Since it's happening in *your* body, you owe it to yourself to do the research and learn as much as you can about your condition. If the molecular biology is too overwhelming, think of it in broader terms, which you should be doing anyway. Let the doctors do their bit, while you and your energy workers do theirs.

It always comes back to the inquiry. Do you feel like there's a blockage, tightness, inflammation? Are you wanting to loosen things up, let something pass through and out? Is there something you're holding onto, from this life or another, which you have to confront or let go of?

You really must—and this is where the imagination comes in—visualize and come to an understanding from the inside out (and the outside in), regarding what is really going on energetically with this disease that has expressed itself in you (or someone else).

Getting further into the nitty gritty of a case study—or several—is beyond the scope of this book. It would certainly be a valid topic for future writings to explore, but I will share a few lists of stones in the following sections that I think will serve as good examples of ones that could be helpful to consider when you're suffering.

Stress & Anxiety

This is one of the number one concerns for people and a frequent reason they inquire about stones. Doctors will tell you that it's also the number one threat to your health. If you're under pressure and overreacting (or reacting appropriately, given the circumstances), it's hard to rest and digest well. Insomnia happens and a host of maladies gather overhead, like clouds.

Life can seem burdensome when you're always overwhelmed and in a worst-case scenario, some consider suicide. I know for myself—in retrospect, after several close calls with death—that my own body was saying, "If this is what life is like, I want out." That's what happens when you're not happy. There are many ways to self-harm and getting sick is certainly one of them.

Granted, getting sick is not always a reactive or corrective response to our eating poorly, staying in a bad relationship, or putting up with the wrong job. Sometimes it just happens. No fault, it's genetics, or bad luck. Of course, there are those who believe there is no bad luck, that we are entirely responsible for our own reality. But you have to have a little understanding, a little mercy, and accept sometimes what is (and shows up) without having to seek blame for it.

Also, it might not be bad fortune or circumstances that are eating away at us. Some people have a lot more nervous energy than others. It could be intrinsic or the result of trauma. They don't necessarily have more, or even any seriously life-threatening stressors. But being hypervigilant, anything can set them off. Our own stress and anxiety hormones could be poisoning us.

However we got here, we're here nonetheless, feeling stressed out and anxious. What can the Crystal World offer that helps? As it happens, there are many options. If budget is a consideration, here are

IMAGE 89   VOICE

AQUAMARINE crystal, dark blue (Vietnam), more on page 158

Higher Mind, the Writers' Stone

some lower-end options. Unless another color calls to you, I recommend greens and blues.

Easy small tumblers that are soothing and good to have around (larger sizes okay too):

- ✧ **Green New Jade** (very soothing, similar to Nephrite Jade, but blue sometimes) — **HEART**
- ✧ **Green Chert** (not even on my main lists, but another facsimile of Nephrite Jade) — **HEART**
- ✧ **Green Calcite** (best for this purpose in a smaller size, can look just like New Jade) — **HEALING**
- ✧ **Angelite** (very soothing baby blue) — **HEALING**
- ✧ **Blue Lace Agate** (replete with dreamy and beautiful layers) — **HEALING**
- ✧ **Chrysocolla** (combines Turquoise and Malachite, confers humility and self-forgiveness) — **VOICE**

Some more primary (heavy duty) stones for stress and anxiety are:

- ✧ **Ruby, Meteorite, Hematite, Garnet** (all good for Grounding) — **ROOT**
- ✧ **Lavender Fluorite** (for instant Calming of the nervous system) — **HEALING**
- ✧ **Malachite** (like having a steam release, letting your feelings out, good for a cry) — **HEART**
- ✧ **Smoky Quartz** (letting go of what you're holding onto, detoxifying & forgiveness) — **HEART**
- ✧ **Nephrite Jade** (soothing, providing a sense of larger context and the embrace of mother earth) — **HEART**
- ✧ **Lavender Chalcedony** (restoring alignment)— **HEALING**

VOICE IMAGE 90

CHRYSOCOLLA egg (Peru), more on page 159

Self Respecting Humility

What do you do with these stones? Let us count the ways! Meditation, carrying them around with you, wearing appropriate jewelry, setting up intentional layouts or constellations, or seeking the guidance and support of a practitioner like myself. Any or all of these can be helpful.

Once you start thinking about your situation in spiritual terms (you don't even have to be unwell to do this), it becomes possible to identify and concretize the concepts and issues you're facing, and to address them using particular stones. This helps us process what's happening inside and gives us an edge and an opportunity to get out in front of whatever challenge we may be facing.

Surgery

It's come to this. You're going to have surgery. What crystals are useful when anticipating such a radical intervention (and assault on your aura)? I created a video about this on YouTube and a follow-up one that I found relevant for *after* surgery. Here's what I said...

Whether it's you or someone you know, going under the knife is a scary prospect. I've identified ten crystals I think will make it a better (and ideally safer) experience.

1. **Ruby** (for direct stone grounding into the earth, a source of sustenance and security) — **ROOT**
2. **Topaz** (to communicate with and prepare your body, I call it the body whisperer) — **VOICE**
3. **Water Rose Quartz** (for cleansing, letting go of that which no longer serves you) — **HEALING**
4. **Carnelian** (for improved bowel/organ function, which is generally impacted by surgical interventions) — **BELLY**
5. **Rhodochrosite** (for cellular repair and regeneration) — **ROOT**

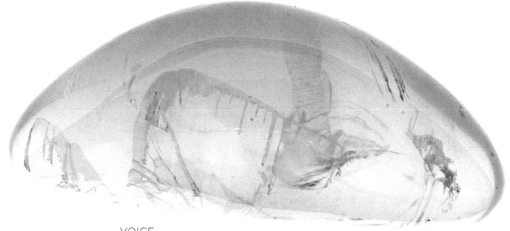

IMAGE 91   VOICE

GIRASOL aka FOGGY QUARTZ freeform
(Madagascar), more on page 159
Trust & Faith in the Unknown

6. **Lavender Chalcedony** (for realignment and healing) — HEALING

7. **Foggy** or **Girasol Quartz** (for trust and faith in the unknown) — VOICE

8. **Celestite** (for heavenly mercies) — HEALING

9. **Morion Smoky Quartz** (for protection, being watched over when you are hospitalized or home and vulnerable) — CHANNEL

10. **Angled transmitter Quartz crystal** (to project and receive connection and intention around your caretakers) — CHANNEL

The above don't even consider your spirit guides or other connections and supplications you may wish to make to the higher forces, for which I recommend Source and Channel stones in general (as facilitators, and for seeking succor).

I've found that what you need *after* a surgical intervention can be radically different, but complementary, to what you need *before* surgery (when you have the luxury of approaching it more dispassionately). Read the descriptions of the following stones to see how these are different. They are kinder and gentler because of your increased vulnerability after procedures.

1. **Calcite** (a soft healer and binder, to match your frailty, meet you where you're at) — HEALING

2. **Butterscotch Amber** to absorb pain, prepare for healing) — HEALING

3. **Green Prehnite** (known as the stone aloe vera, for external soothing of the body surface) — HEALING

4. **Pink Chalcedony** (for a loving resealing and internal realignment) — HEALING

5. **Chrysocolla** (for self-compassion, humility, gratitude toward others) — VOICE

VOICE   IMAGE 92

BLUE JADEITE rough tumbler (Guatemala), more on page 160

Honesty and Truth

6. **Milky Quartz** (for compassion to and from all) — HEART

7. **Cobalto Calcite** or **pink Fluorite** (love healing, healing the heart) — HEALING

8. **Red Petrified Wood** (revitalization from below, to get your energy back) — ROOT

All of the post-surgical stones hail from the Healing energy zone except two. Chrysocolla comes from Voice, as you call out for help and are forced to go easy on yourself. And the Red Petrified Wood, which is from the Root zone, is there to give you a boost as you look to regain your strength.

Maintaining Wellness

I think it's important to note that working with crystals is not meant to be a substitute or an override for common sense and best practices when it comes to your health. Good diet and exercise are obviously essential. That being said, these are crystals I recommend as good touchstones for maintaining your wellness.

1. **Topaz** (essential for staying in constant communication with your body) — VOICE

2. **Ruby** (your connection to the earth, you want to remain grounded at all times) — ROOT

3. **Carnelian** (for being specifically in touch with your body functions) — BELLY

4. **Herkimer Diamond** (for keeping strong in the fortress that is you) — HEALING

5. **Lavender Chalcedony** (for staying in alignment, not stressing out) — HEALING

6. **Rhodochrosite** (for regenerative vitality) — ROOT

IMAGE 93   VOICE

VONSEN BLUE JADE rough tumbler (USA), more on page 160

A different Perspective

Death

This world is ultimately a playground for the living, who carry their torch through a world that was originally built by and already experienced by the dead. After taking our own turn, we each step off the carousel. Whether we go into oblivion or another life, we may never know for certain. It's the responsibility of the survivors to honor the dead and to send them off with proper ritual and acknowledgment.

I have a Guatemalan clay frog-shaped whistle that I blow into—as if in a call and response—to echo the last breath of the departed. I think there are some stones that are worth bringing into play as well. Here's a list of six that I think are relevant

1. **Bedrock, Granite** or any such common stone (for our return to the elements) — **FOUNDATION**

2. **Entity Stone** (to reflect the disembodied spirit and to help it find its new home) — CHANNEL

3. **Emerald** (for the deeper love that is immortalized on someone's passing) — **HEART**

4. **Crystal Skull**, any material (to represent what lives on and keep the connection) — CHANNEL

5. **Green Fluorite** (for the liminal waiting room and spirit community they pass through) — SOURCE

6. **Nirvana Quartz** (for their having passed into the ages, joining all generations) — SOURCE

VOICE   IMAGE 94

BLUE KYANITE gemmy cluster (Brazil), more on page 160

The Grounded Voice

THINGS WE SEEK

Beyond health, much of what we seek in life has to do with the outside world—things we aspire to, or would like to bring more of into our lives.

Love & Relationships

"What crystal is good for love?" This one always comes up and, as ever, this type of question is hard to answer because it's so unspecific. I know what's meant though. Someone's looking for love, a romantic relationship. And they want me to give them a fix-it stone that will suddenly bring Mr., Ms. (or whatever pronoun you like) Right into their lives.

While there are many who'll be quick to give you that easy answer, I'm prone to counter, as usual, with some back-atcha questions. To answer intelligently, we both need these answers.

This thing you're seeking is outside of you, but you have to start with the love within, for yourself. Are you even ready to be in a relationship? Do you know what you're looking for? Are you willing to make the compromises necessary to make it work? I'm no matchmaker or couple's counselor, so I can't take you further down this particular road of questioning, but I recommend you look into their services to help you navigate this aspect of your journey.

For my part, I always consider the big picture so, as you read on, remember that when I hear the word love, I'm thinking macro. You'll notice that the six stones I've picked below, which I think are particularly relevant for relationships, hail from Voice, Heart, and Self.

IMAGE 95   VOICE

LAPIS chunk, top quality (Afghanistan), more on page 160

Finding and Using your Voice

- ✧ **Chrysocolla** (engenders the capacity to resist harsh judgement of others and self) — **VOICE**

- ✧ **Smoky Quartz** (allows you to let go of the past, and forgive more easily in the present) — **HEART**

- ✧ **Rose Quartz** (tells the world "I'm here" and ready to receive, with unconditional love) — **HEART**

- ✧ **Lepidolite** (lets you feel the contact point with those you get along with and not so much) — **HEART**

◇ **Pyrite** (helps you keep healthy boundaries from within, what is me and what is not me) — SELF

◇ **Girasol**, or **Foggy Quartz** (cultivates trust and faith in the process and the universe) — VOICE

Abundance / Prosperity

VOICE   IMAGE 96

LAZULITE chunk (Brazil),
more on page 161

The Measured Tone

I'm not going to tell you I have the key to wealth or how to make money. Everybody gets there (or doesn't) using their own unique path. Some will tell you they've got it all figured out and if you just buy their program, you too can have what they have. What they're doing is selling the dream. People will pay a lot of money to follow that rainbow. I'm not telling you they won't produce the desired outcome, or that they're ripping you off, but always remember that it's really just a dream that you're paying for. Ultimately it's *you* who has to make that dream into a reality.

The word "success" tends to mean one thing in this society: money (and lots of it). There are some good people who'll tell you (and it's easy to show you, taking one glimpse at the environment) that endless growth, and the way we've pursued it for these past several hundreds of years (at least), is killing the planet. Our current economic model and its obsession with expansion is probably unsustainable. This could be because capitalism is not a natural occurrence. It is an artificial entity, fabricated after the start of agriculture to manage and grow what we have come to call civilizations.

This is why I respect the Indigenous peoples who walked these continents for tens of thousands of years in a perfectly sustainable fashion. When the Europeans arrived, they stamped all over this worldview, having tasted the riches that were possible through colonialism. And now it seems that regardless of ideology, even communist countries operate by the same rules of greed and dominion.

I'm not trying to get political. People think, "Oh, you're going there? I thought this book was about crystals!" Yes, this book is about crystals, but we don't live in a bubble. Pandemics and illness don't care about politics, neither does climate change. We ignore the impact of our human presence and policies at our own peril.

Now let's get back to abundance and prosperity. You have to think outside the artificial box of dollars and cents. How do those concepts appear in the wild? Abundance means having more than enough. Prosperity means favorable, fortunate, or having good luck. Because we've associated those words with money, I think it's relevant to note that beyond a certain amount to cover your basic expenses annually, having millions and pursuing billions does not make you any more happy.

There's something other than sheer dollars that's more directly associated with happiness.

I would tie happiness and the experience of abundance and prosperity to satisfaction and fulfillment. To experience *those* things, I believe we have to move away from the rat race and culture of perpetual not-enoughness to start appreciating what we have more readily.

IMAGE 97   VOICE

SUGILITE large rainbow chunk (South Africa), more on page 162
The Manifestation Stone

I'm not talking about settling or not striving for better, just about being more appreciative along the way. Stop judging yourself and others for where we each find ourselves on the highway of life. This goal may be pursued through gratitude, by being thankful and counting our blessings.

Have a look at my list of recommended stones in this arena, and see how they reflect some of what I've said above.

- ✧ **Celestite** (appreciate what you have with this stone of gratitude and heavenly gifts) — HEALING

- ✧ **Rhodochrosite** (get in touch with the fulfillment you want to experience, energetically) — ROOT

- ✧ **Pyrite** (respect your boundaries, identify and get what you need without being greedy) — SELF

- ✧ **Lapis** (ask for what you want, find and use your voice to advocate for yourself) — **VOICE**

- ✧ **Sugilite** (get clear about your vision, engage in bringing it forward to being a reality) — **VOICE**

- ✧ **Ventifact** (pursue your passion unabashedly, let it open doors for you, remove obstacles) — **CHANNEL**

You may have noticed that some stones appear on multiple lists. That's only natural, as they have energy that's relevant to multiple areas. I could add more stones, but I'm trying to keep it as simple as possible. I want nonetheless to provide a multidimensional view of the options available for engaging constructively with these various spheres of life.

VOICE   IMAGE 98

TOPAZ natural generator crystal (Brazil), more on page 163

The Body Whisperer

Creative Energy / Manifestation

We all wish we had more hours in the day, more energy to get things done during our waking hours. To that end, we take stimulants to work and sedatives to sleep. This has us losing touch with our own natural rhythms, which I think is antithetical to having our systems generating consistently good energy.

According to my understanding of crystals, the more we can get back to nature with our own consciousness, the better. When we settle into a meditation, we don't want our head buzzing with caffeine. We don't want the stones we work with to feel like just another prescription or a pill.

Here are some recommended stones for energy.

- ✧ **Herkimer Diamond** (for strength) — **HEALING**

- ✧ **Ruby** (for leaping off a solid foundation) — **ROOT**

- ✧ **Dragon Quartz** (for kindling a fire under your butt) — **ROOT**

- ✧ **White Opal** (for a strong internal orientation point) — HEALING

- ✧ **Petrified Wood**, all types (to help you make things happen in the world) — **FOUNDATION**, **ROOT**, SELF

What do we do if we're in a creative rut? Say we need a hit of imagination. I know it's tempting, but it's not practical for us to take hallucinogens to get our creative juices flowing. What we need is to get in touch with our Vision energy zone and to power it from our Root through our Voice.

- ✧ **Obsidian & Jet** (to clear the slate, both outside and inside, starting fresh) — CHANNEL, HEALING

- ✧ **Dark Amethyst** (identify your spiritual mission, what you're really here to achieve) — **VISION**

- ✧ **Labradorite** or colorful **Opal** (start thinking outside the box, receive the brainstorm) — **VISION**

- ✧ **Clear & Laser Quartz** (get clarity and focus about your intentions to make a plan) — CHANNEL

- ✧ **Sugilite** (activate the process of realization, taking it from a vision to a reality) — **VOICE**

IMAGE 99   VOICE

TURQUOISE plate (Mexico), more on page 163

Self-Forgiveness

Ascension

Ascension is the highest level we can achieve, personally and collectively. It's not just a personal high, although for many, that might feel like enough. Reaching those levels just for the fun of it feels kind of empty, and out of context. True ascension is not just a selfish bliss.

It's challenging though. Even though we are ultimately social beings, it's sometimes hard to feel connected when on some levels, we are born, live, and die alone. The fact that your mother was there at your birth, and people tend to you once you've passed on may not be reassuring at all. Getting lost in our aloneness is part of what makes being human tough.

What makes being human transcendent, however, are acts of kindness, giving, and compassion. The Oxford Dictionary defines a Bodhisattva as "a person who is able to reach nirvana but delays doing so out of compassion, in order to save suffering beings." It is beautiful and honorable to think that our ultimate fulfillment consists of our capacity to not simply seize the prize for ourselves, but to actually share it and invite everyone else to the table.

I think that's what should be motivating us. With this as a supreme directive, we can save the world and all of us in it. Anything else may be just vanity and destruction.

That being said, how do we get there? Here are 10 stone suggestions for both elevation and connection.

- ✧ **Apophyllite** (the ascension stone, takes us up 50 flights in an instant) — CHANNEL
- ✧ **Green, Blue and Aquamarine Fluorite** (integrates us into the spirit community, be it above or deeply beneath the surface) — SOURCE
- ✧ **Pyrite Concretions** (allows us to connect with underground earth spirits) — SOURCE
- ✧ **Moldavite** (allows us to receive the messages and directives from on high) — SOURCE
- ✧ **Lemurian Quartz** (invites us to take on the mantle of our highest spiritual identity) — SOURCE
- ✧ **Nirvana Quartz** (joins us into the company of the ascended masters) — SOURCE
- ✧ **Auralite** (connects us through the ages, forward and backward through time) — **FOUNDATION**
- ✧ **Milky Quartz** (allows us to experience the benevolence of the universe) — HEART
- ✧ **Chevron Amethyst** (enables us to merge compassion with charity) — HEALING
- ✧ **Nephrite Jade** (connects us with, and back to Mother Earth) — HEART

✧ ✧ ✧

And that does it! These lists I've provided for you are not meant to be sexhaustive or exclusive. You can add others as necessary, but these lists are sufficient to give you plenty to work with and to help you better understand the subtle and complex energies that each of our life challenges involves.

VISION   IMAGE 100

PATTERNED AGATE display piece (Brazil), more on page 164

Creative Possibilities

Part 3

THE STONES

Stone Listing by Energy Zone

Please note (regarding this and the following two-category listing):

✧ These lists are not meant to be exhaustive, you won't find every stone under the sun here

✧ Stones whose names are bold are in our latest meditation and affirmation card deck (2018)

✧ Some feature a phrase in parentheses which speaks to the stone's essential qualities

✧ Some instead or additionally feature an italic phrase, which may be used for contemplation

✧ The images throughout the book have summary/variations of the descriptions above

✧ Some stones I have only a general sense of, because I'm still researching and learning about them

✧ If I haven't enough to say about a stone, it might only appear in the two-category list that follows

✧ You may find inconsistencies in my alphabetization, but there is some logic to it

✧ In the future, I may have more or different things to say about many of these, as my perspectives evolve

✧ What's here is supplemented and updated on my main website, as well as through my social media posts, blogs, podcasts, and YouTube/TikTok videos

Amazez

Compassionate Oversight
(Angelic Guardians)

A pale semi-Chevron Amethyst (alternately lighter-purple-then-white layers), named by Robert Simmons, I believe. It's akin to Auralite but it's lighter, less heavy-handed energetically. Amazez would be very helpful to invoke and involve spirit guides for particular undertakings.

IMAGE 1 **Amazez** page 4

Ammonite

Be in the Presence of All That Has Moved
(All Generations, Animal Life)

Sixty-million-year-old seafaring nautiloid fossils found in Morocco and Madagascar, sometimes with pearly or interestingly formed shells that have lent themselves well to being cut in half so you can see the intricate formation of their insides. I like how all stages of their life are on display, from when they were tiny till when they reached maturity.

IMAGE 2 **Ammonite** page 5

VISION   IMAGE 101

DYED AGATE disc (Brazil), more on page 164
Appearances

Auralite

Generational Layers
(Past Lives, You and Yours)

Officially called Auralite-23 due to the many elements it supposedly contains. I'm not that interested in that aspect of their composition. What I care about is the rich layering of one Amethyst cluster atop an-other over millennia and how this layering symbolizes us looking back on both human (flesh and blood) and spiritual ancestors. Another nuance of this stone is how it invites us to look back on the earlier stages of our own life. Past life regression or an effort to heal trauma with your elders and your younger self invite Auralite to get involved.

IMAGE 3 **Auralite** page 6 + 174

Bedrock

The Stone That the Builder Refused is the Head Cornerstone
(Foundation of the Planet)

Granite or other such common stones get this blanket term: Bedrock. I used to discount this entire class of stones as irrelevant, preferring stones that had crystallized or were otherwise evolved enough to have a more uniform and distinguished content (like Lapis or Angelite). I was wrong. How could the rest of the stone world, which is under our feet and comprises every continent, be meaningless? Bedrock is to be respected and revered. In meditations, I often invite us to place ourselves on the land where we are, on the planet as a whole. We ultimately lie on (and rely on) the bedrock!

IMAGE 4 **Bedrock** page 7

Brecciated Jasper

A patterned version of red Jasper, it's an interesting variety worth checking out. It's as if a fossil met Jasper, but without being biological in origin. It's got intricate patterning and is one of the many Jasper varieties known for their distinctive patterning.

Coquina Jasper

Resting Place of the Ages

Also known as Script or Meriam Stone, and one of my favorites: Hieroglyphic Jasper. Impressive not only because of its number of names, but because this stone

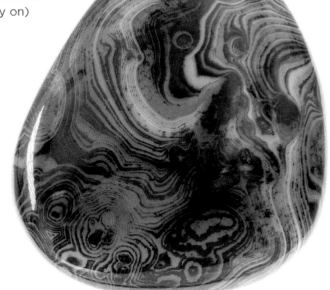

IMAGE 102   VISION

MYSTIC AGATE (Madagascar), more on page 164
The Genius of Dreams

VISION   IMAGE 103

DARK AMETHYST twin points (Brazil), more on page 165
Spiritual Mission

is truly amazing to look at. It's like a fossil particle-board. Bits of yellowish-orange bone are jumbled together in a deeper reddish-orange ochre matrix. Differently from the single organism Ammonites, I think this material speaks to the collective mix of past lives in the ground, immortalized in this petrified blend.

IMAGE 5 **Coquina Jasper** page 9

Dinosaur Gembone

When Giants Walked the Earth
(Prehistoric Royalty)

Unlike a garden variety fossil bone, Gembone has been replaced by minerals that not only petrify it but also beautify it, giving the intricate bone marrow cells color and vibrancy. This lends itself to Dino Gembone being used for jewelry and commanding increasingly higher prices. Apparently, like Petrified Wood itself, you can no longer mine it on public land. It is most appreciated in rich reds, but it also comes in lighter varieties.

IMAGE 6 **Dinosaur Gembone** sphere page 10

Elestial Quartz

Wisdom of the Ages
(The Elders)

Different from Auralite, the Elestials have a more individual personality and identity. They are like a physical embodiment of the collective, including our outstanding ancestors and descendants, connected through time and space. We evoke them when we want to honor them and we invite them to witness and support us in the present. Brazilians call these Jacaré, or Alligator Quartz, because its surface is broken up and resembles reptile skin.

IMAGE 7 **Elestial Quartz** page 11

Fossils

Be in the Presence of All That Has Moved
(All Generations, Animal Life)

These are represented by Ammonite in my Crystal Concentrics Meditation and Affirmation card deck. You'll notice the same energetic explanation for this as for the Ammonite. Any fossil can evoke this association. Some are more interesting and evocative to look at.

IMAGE 2 **Ammonite**, representative of fossils page 5

Petrified Wood, black

Petrified Woods come in a variety of colors. This one is foundational, a black version of bedrock.

Pinolith

The Inanimate Lives!

Also called Pinolite, it's found in Europe and Canada. It looks organic but it's not. Makes for beautiful sculpture and jewelry, as it is composed of spiky white crystals jumbled together (and looking biological) in a black matrix.

IMAGE 8 **Pinolith** page 12

Stromatolite

Honoring the Herbal Essences
(All Generations of Plant Life)

I featured the attractive green spotted Kambaba Jasper variety in my card deck, which is from Madagascar. You can also get more rustic, sandy-looking types from Morocco and a wavy brown type from Peru (another favorite of mine).

IMAGE 9 **Kambaba Jasper** stromatolite page 13

IMAGE 104   VISION

BLUE APATITE sphere (Madagascar),
more on page 69 + 165

The Unconscious

2. ROOT — LIFE FORCE

Dragon Quartz

Doing and Being Energy
(Life Fire)

Of the three types that originate from Morocco, this is my favorite red iron-coated Quartz. I use it to conjure life energy. Its clusters most resemble a dragon's spiky skin. There was a time when it was more prevalent, but I believe they can't find any more. What I like about it is that its crystals look like they're falling over each other and that the red color is not just on the surface (like it is with the other varieties), it seems baked in and permeating all the crystals.

IMAGE 10 **Dragon Quartz** page 14

Edenite

Tapping the Spring
(Emergent Plant Life)

I originally nicknamed this Green Rutilated Quartz, although it's definitely not metallic Rutile running through it. Found in the 1990's, I haven't seen any new sourcing of this material, which is unique in two ways. First, it's got what looks like green Rutile (or blades of grass) running through it. Some say it might be Actinolite, but we haven't had it tested to know for sure. Second, it's sometimes a natural laser, shaped like the Diamantina Quartz of Brazil. I like to use this to tap into the power of the season of spring each year. I've only ever seen literally a handful of these.

IMAGE 11 **Edenite laser Quartz** page 15

VISION | IMAGE 105

INDIGO FLUORITE chunk (China), more on page 166

Twilight without Judgement

Galena

Crystallizes into various forms. One I like a lot makes it look like little pueblos, boxes all on top of one another. It's nice visually, as specimens, and that form certainly has metaphorical value, but I prefer Hematite over it. Also, I might be a bit put off by the fact that it's mostly lead, which is not healthy for humans. Still, it makes for nice specimen display pieces.

I have a funny story about Galena. A guy drove somewhere to buy hundreds of pounds of Galena and was told, "It's around back, in the yard." The guy looked but couldn't find it. He went up front and asked where it was. The owner laughed: "It was a pile 20 years ago when I bought it, now it's all sunk into the ground!"

Garnet

A glassy version of Ruby, Garnet makes for a wonderful grounding stone, particularly if it's a natural circular crystal (or cut/faceted to look like one). The only reason I prefer Ruby is that it's stonier, and says "grounding" a bit more loudly. My wife wears a Garnet stretchy bracelet, which she finds quite grounding too, although the dark red shows up black in video conferences. You'd be hard pressed to find a comparable (or bright red) Ruby bracelet that's not a fortune. So Garnet's often the better jewelry choice.

Hematite

Isness and Flow
(Metallic Grounding)

I'm a big fan of Hematite. It offers more than grounding. Being somewhat uniform inside and metallic (like Copper, which is a good conductor of electricity), I find that it also connects us universally. That's a great second feature to boast. While most commonly found tumbled, it has great botryoidal (bubbly) terminations out of Morocco, and can also form very distinctive semi-geometric crystals that look like twisted steel.

IMAGE 12 geometric abstract **Hematite** page 16 and botrioidal version page 172

IMAGE 106   VISION

OCEAN JASPER sphere (Madagascar),
more on page 69 + 166

The Inventiveness of Nature

Iron Meteorite

*Toward the Center of
the Earth*
(Grounding from Space)

The only thing stopping these from heading straight to the center of the earth was our planet's surface. Think of these as coming to us on a trajectory that directly connects the universe with our own earth's core. It has more power, in a way, than Hematite because the grounding is extended downwards *and* upwards. It's like a great big anchor or rudder, very stabilizing!

VISION   IMAGE 107

LABRADORITE palm piece (Madagascar),
more on page 167

Imagination, Gateway to the Subsconscious

The main varieties I use most are from Campo del Cielo in Argentina and Sikhote Alin from Siberia. The American Diablo Canyon meteorites tend to rust, which makes them more of a geological specialty. I am personally very drawn to the Graphite-like Nantan meteorites from China. And there are others: Gibeon from Namibia and Muonionalusta from Finland are other well-known meteorites.

IMAGE 13 large **Campo del Cielo Meteorite** page 17

Jasper, red

Keep it Steady
(Balanced Life Force)

This is a quiet giant. It doesn't get the love or admiration many other stones do, but it's steady as a rock, imparting a sense of equilibrium. I recommend palm-ish sized pieces for meditation or display pieces for a room. I like polished just about as much as rough on these.

IMAGE 14 **Red Jasper** page 18

Obsidian, mahogany

While Black Obsidian is a channel stone devoted to openness, the orange that flows through Mahogany Obsidian brings its energy down to the Root. It's not one of my favorite Obsidians, but I respect it and recognize that it's one of those stones I need to learn more about. One of my shamanic friends swears by it!

Opal, satin flash

Blazing through the Ages

Quite an obscure variety—I know of only one source for it—an extinct geyser in Utah that went dry 18,000 years ago. Still, it's got such an extraordinary look, like a huge wall of flames, that I found it a shoo-in for inclusion here in Root. When oiled it looks more orange, but when left natural it has a much more pale look (like the flames are spiritual).

IMAGE 15 **Satin Flash Opal** page 19

Petrified Wood, red

Getting Things Going
(Fire Down Below)

Red Petrified Wood is my favorite, actually, but I use them all. This one is similar in energy signature to Dragon Quartz but more elemental (basic). Very helpful for people who have been unwell and need more Chi, Dantien, or Hara (life energy and vitality). I think it would be good to put under one's bed to ignite other passions as well.

IMAGE 16 **Arizona Red Petrified Wood** page 20

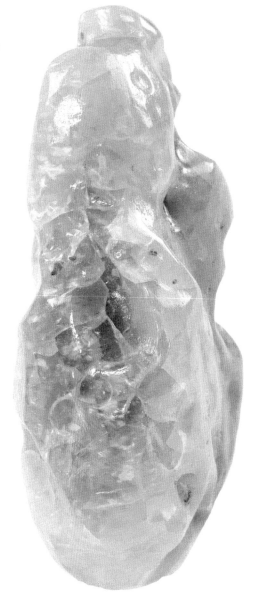

IMAGE 108   VISION

ETHIOPIAN OPAL floater palm piece (Ethiopia), more on page 168
Infinite Possibilities

Red Cap Amethyst

Where the Unmanifest Meets the Manifest
(Sourcing from Beneath)

Also known as Super Seven, type 2. I love this stuff. It's definitely Amethyst, because of the shape, but the body is basically Smoky and the cap is red (not purple). Found only in Brazil. It's like an umbilical cord from the earth, which bridges the physically unmanifest to the conceived and born. This stone is where the rubber meets the road because it speaks to the place where Spirit has connected with the material world, like the wheels of a jet plane when it touches down.

IMAGE 17 **Red Cap Amethyst** page 21

VISION   IMAGE 109

SERAPHINITE fan display piece (Russia), more on page 169
Discovering the Unknown

Red Laser Quartz

Harnessed Life Energy
(Focused Fire)

Found mostly between 2010-15, I have not seen anything since, so I'm glad I've stockpiled a bunch of this material. None of the myriad Madagascar dealers have ever carried it, even though it comes from there. I got it through China. Like Edenite and the Diamantinas from Brazil, these are naturally tapered lasers. It's the only other place in the world where this happens. Very good for funneling life energy into specific areas.

IMAGE 18 **Red Laser Quartz** page 22

Rhodochrosite

May I Be Renewed
(Cellular Vitality)

One of my favorites for sure, I'm particularly enamored of the gemmy red material from both Argentina and Peru (where it has a different look and feel). I'm seeing the rich colored variety less and less at the big shows. The pale stuff being sold instead is just not as interesting or vibrationally relevant. Great for physical recovery, simplistically associated with fertility, but all around a good stone for (and resembling the) healthy flesh.

IMAGE 19 botryoidal **Rhodochrosite**, with cross section page 23 and large heart page 182

Rhodonite

Supporting Possibility

The little sister of Rhodochrosite! Makes for nice jewelry and cool to have around, but not nearly as strong as Rhodochrosite. Mostly from Brazil, it's found in bubble gum pink to darker pink with black splotches. Some people resonate more with it than Rhodochrosite. It's companion capacity to Rhodochrosite helped me arrive at its descriptor "Supporting Possibility."

IMAGE 20 **Rhodonite** page 24

IMAGE 110   VISION

SHATTUCKITE polished rough (Congo), more on page 169
Shield of the Subsconscious

Ruby

Starting Point, Home Base
(Stone Grounding)

This is the ultimate grounding stone, the stone's stone. Starts being useful at palm size, though nice in pendants if you use bigger/cheaper pieces. It is often dyed in cheap jewelry and too expensive (not energetically practical) once you get into the higher grades. People are surprised at how brownish red the lower grade material is, but that's where I think the mojo is to be found (in the lower grades, larger pieces).

IMAGE 21 **Ruby** page 25

Stibnite

Grows in elongated, gray metallic crystals. I've never had occasion to use this material, but it can be beautiful and makes me think of a more focused flow if you wanted to make Hematite into a wand. I believe it comes primarily from China, and while much of it can look like stuck together spaghetti, the more valuable specimens are clean rods.

Tiger Iron

Blended Roots
(Rooted Flow)

This combines the grounding of Hematite, the balance of red Jasper, and the self-reflective quality of Tiger Eye. A good thing to have around for a more complex grounding experience.

IMAGE 22 standing **Tiger Iron** free form page 26

SOURCE   IMAGE 111

AREA 51 STONE Dolomite over Aragonite (USA),
more on page 170

Relics of Visitation

3. BELLY — ORGANS

Carnelian

My Body's Making It Happen
(Automatic Functions)

I really like Carnelian. It's like a deeper, more biological Agate. They're both essentially Quartz Chalcedony, but this one has more vibes. Colors range from brown to orange, red to yellow. It symbolizes all the internal organs and functioning, the way our body knows what to do with digestion, glands, hormone regulation, and so much more.

IMAGE 23 rich colored **Carnelian** nugget page 27

"Citrine" (faux)

Useful Transformation
(Cooking It Through)

Also known as baked Amethyst, this used to be my nemesis because I was so annoyed that people continued to sell it as the real thing. True Citrine is a Self stone, while this is a Belly stone. They really aren't the same.

I have always appreciated its beauty. In Brazil, when it's gem cut and dark, it's called Rio Grande Do Sul Citrine. What I like about my energetic description above is that I was able to find a use for this stone, which represents how we can force changes on ourselves in a good and productive way. It symbolizes our capacity to take situations and make the best of them. We eat all kinds of things, yet our body knows how to break them all down and digest them, putting their energies where they are needed.

There is a variety of this I'd like to make you aware of. It's called Ouro Verde or Green Gold Citrine in Brazil. It does have a slightly green hue and is treated to reach an almost perfect Citrine color. It's found mostly in jewelry, unlike Lemon Citrine, which is more of an unnatural yellow. Unfortunately, all these false Citrines have flooded the market, and it's easier to think you're buying the real thing than ever.

IMAGE 24 top grade **faux Citrine** cluster page 28

IMAGE 112   SOURCE

ASTROPHYLLITE obelisk (Russia),
more on page 171

Shooting Stars' Reflection

Green Opal

Honoring All Parts
(Individual Organs)

Dedicated to all the major and minor organs and glands within. It's odd to have a green stone in this energy zone, but here you have it. Putting it here was an inspiration. I prefer these darker in color. The lighter ones do less for me, but some people find them attractive.

IMAGE 25 **Green Opal** page 29

Mango Quartz

Nourishing Passage

This is another rarity from Madagascar, basically an Amphibole Quartz, where gauzy, cloudy, colorful inclusions appear throughout their inside, giving the crystal a yellow/pink/orange color. I actually find it a more powerful but obscure version of Orange Calcite. Good as a body/organ soother.

IMAGE 26 **Mango Quartz** page 30

Orange Calcite

May I have Ease of Flow
(Body Soothing)

This is the gentle backup to Carnelian. It's like Carnelian is doing the dirty work and heavy lifting, while this does the easy work. Very pleasant and soothing.

IMAGE 27 **Orange Calcite** sphere page 31

Peach Moonstone

Gorgeous stuff, far more common than the rare white Rainbow Moonstone. I have it placed here in Belly, but I've never worked with it. It's on my list of stones to learn more about, energetically.

Tangerine Quartz

Calm Coating

It feels like the Jasper of the 2nd energy zone, very balanced and equilibrium-inducing. It's hard to find great pieces, but I'm grateful to have come across several. Nice to have around.

IMAGE 28 **Tangerine Quartz** page 32

IMAGE 114   SOURCE

CELESTIAL QUARTZ floater/shard (Brazil), more on page 172

Beam up to the Stratosphere

Ametrine

Balancing Personal and Spiritual
(Self-Realization)

A mix of Citrine and Amethyst, this is a perfect example of a multi-zone stone. The Citrine hails from here in the Self energy zone and the Purple Amethyst hails from Vision, yet they're combined in one stone. Hence the message above, about combining the personal and the spiritual. Dark Amethyst is all about spiritual mission. Even though it's a multi-chakra stone, it defaults to Self because its overall function is more relevant to the Self.

IMAGE 29 large cathedralized **Ametrine** generator/transmitter page 33, etched page 173 and obelisk page 179

Aragonite, crystallized

Cool stuff. It either appears as a kind of amorphous foamy white cluster (also labeled Calcite) from Mexico or a defined double terminated or starburst crystal (with flat, six-sided points) from Spain and Morocco respectively. Both feel like they're sourcing energy and sharing it, a bit like Golden Rutilated Quartz.

Aventurine

At Home with the Self

A simple green Quartz, it never crystallizes but is still nice to have around. It can sometimes be called Jade (by unscrupulous vendors) and is used as a cheaper alternative for carving deities than real Jade. My favorite form is uniformly colored chunks, like the one whose photo is featured here in this book. Mind you, Aventurine comes in other colors, most notably orange, and the Tanzurines (green and red) are essentially Aventurines.

IMAGE 30 **Green Aventurine** chunk page 34

SOURCE   IMAGE 115

CHRYSANTHEMUM STONE display piece (China), more on page 173

Starbeams from Home

Blue/Black Tiger Eye

Reflection on the Inner Self
(Deep Introspection)

Also known as Hawk's Eye. This is a newly discovered stone for me. I've always known about it, but I finally meditated with it a few times and ended up bringing it into my Self energy zone curriculum class. As Tiger Eye is a favorable reflection on your best aspects, this dark Tiger Eye is an opportunity to look within. No judgment, being totally and transparently authentic with what's going on. The name Hawk's Eye is used often interchangeably, but from photos I've seen, it's a slightly simpler pattern than we're used to from Tiger Eye in general.

Bumblebee Jasper

I've always found the color combination of Bumblebee Jasper (from Indonesia) to be a bit garish and tacky, yet it's popular anyhow. It appears in jewelry, slabs, and polished pieces. My favorite instance of it is in the skull whose photo is featured here in this book. Because of all its patterning, thusly I consider this having Vision qualities, but have assigned it for now as a Self stone whose exact function is TBA.

IMAGE 176 **Bumblebee Jasper** skull page 190

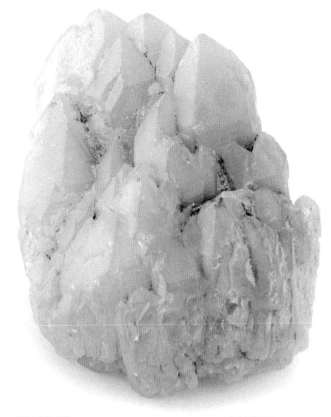

IMAGE 116   SOURCE

DREAM QUARTZ cathedral floater (Madagascar), more on page 173

Spirit Mansions

Citrine

I Am Good As I Am and Will to Be
(Positive Ego, Self)

True, natural Citrine has long been a favorite of mine and many others, who will pay more for it once they learn that the faux Citrine and most jewelry Citrine is treated (and not Citrine at all). There's a lot of Smoky Citrine out there, but as long as you can see that it's distinctly yellow and not brown (by holding a classic Smoky up to it), then it's a Citrine. I consider Citrine to speak for the true and innocent, uncorrupted self.

SOURCE   IMAGE 117

AQUAMARINE FLUORITE blended hearts
(Mexico), more on page 173
Subconscious of the Natural World

Originally, it came mostly from Brazil, but now it's also found in Congo and Zambia (where it's often noticeably darker). The Madagascar Citrine is generally a lower quality (paler) than either of the other sources.

Image 31 natural **Citrine** page 35 + 163, and Smoky Green Citrine page 169

Fluorite, amber

The Maturing Self

Amber Fluorite is darker, almost brown. My favorite occurrence of it was in a stash of geometrically cubic terminated clusters found in China. I haven't spent time with it, metaphysically, but it's so striking that I had to include it (and its image) here in this book.

IMAGE 32 geometric "M.C. Escher" translucent **Amber Fluorite** cluster page 36

Fluorite, yellow

Yellow Fluorite is uncommon. I believe the best source is Argentina. I'm a huge fan and I know it's a Self stone, but I just don't know in what way it interfaces with the self because I haven't spent enough time with this variety yet.

IMAGE 173 **Yellow Fluorite** angel page 184

Golden Rutilated Quartz

Spreading Your Light
(Constructive Pride)

This stone is all about sharing the best you have to offer with the world. Variations are silver-colored and red Rutile, all metallic, but this one is the most significant. It's rare and wonderful to find it in fully formed Quartz crystals, naturally. Similarly to Black Tourmaline, it grows however it likes, in Quartz.

IMAGE 33 **Golden Rutilated Quartz** page 37

Heliodor

From Brazil and Russia, this is a very valuable yellow to greenish crystal that's sort of a high-end Citrine. Imagine a refined essence of that inner, positive, pure self that we experience with Citrine and you'll have Heliodor. Heliodor is a berl, essentially a yellow Emerald.

Hypersthene

The Birthplace of Personal Growth
(The Shadow Self)

When you really look inside—seeing your flaws and foibles—you have the opportunity to embrace them or embark on a path of personal growth to shift those things into a new direction. It has a silly-sounding name that actually means "over strength" in Greek. It's a beautiful chatoyant (plays with light) black, and we see it mostly in jewelry.

IMAGE 34 **Hypersthene** pendant page 38

Manifestation Quartz

Embracing the Child Within

Kind of hard to photograph, these incredible occurrences involve a fully formed crystal inside of another larger crystal. When I originally learned about them, they were called Penetration Quartz. An interim, lesser known name that I prefer is Child Within crystals. I like Child Within because that's really what it looks like and also what it symbolizes for me.

IMAGE 118   SOURCE

BLUE FLUORITE hewn octahedron (USA), more on page 174
Healing to Higher Communication, Alter-Ego of Green

Petrified Wood, darker

I Will Get My Self There
(Worldly Motion)

Very self-empowering. Whether you have functioning legs or not, this is how you get around. It's an outcropping of the self, just as our legs are, and it's how we transport this self around (by whatever means necessary).

IMAGE 35 **darker Petrified Wood**, from the Southern U.S. page 39

Petrified Wood, lighter

Good Work and Good Works
(Impacting the World)

Symbolic of our hands, they do the bidding of the self, making so many things happen (even through keystrokes on a phone or computer). Manual dexterity, excelling in what you do, and doing good in the world. Another valuable outcropping of the self. Nobody else is grouping arms and legs this way, as an outcropping of Self.

SOURCE   IMAGE 119

GREEN FLUORITE record keeper cluster (China), more on page 60 + 174

Spirit Community

IMAGE 36 **lighter Petrified Wood**, from Indonesia page 40

Phantom Quartz

Layers of Your Past

Although phantoms occasionally occur in other types of stone, we'll list them as Quartz because that's the most common occurrence. Fortunately, we have a photo of one because it's pretty hard to explain. Basically, some crystals grow over time and at earlier stages have had other chemical residue (say, a Smoky layer) deposit over an existing point before it grew taller. The end result is one or a series of little "tents" inside of a crystal, all nestled one above the other. I take these to symbolize earlier stages of our own development, in a more personal way than mentioned about the stone Auralite (which can also be thought of as including earlier stages of our own development in it).

IMAGE 161 **Smoky Green Citrine** with at least eight phantoms page 169

Psilomelane

Connecting Aspects of the Self
(Self-Grounding)

This layered combination of manganese oxides looks like wavy black and gray Hematite. Not surprisingly, it derives its name from the Greek for smooth and black. It's the Self zone's own personal grounding stone, combining different aspects of the Self into a blended whole. The name is odd and takes getting used to, but the stone itself is quite wonderful (and also features nicely in jewelry).

IMAGE 37 **Psilomelane** and **Chalcedony** slab page 41

Pyrite

Owning Your Space
(My Domain)

Some call this Fool's Gold—I prefer to call it Wise One's Gold because it's all about keeping your soul— not losing it in an attempt to gain the world. Pyrite is the shield and fortress of the true self (sort of the protective shield of Citrine). It's how we define best where we leave off and the world picks up. It helps us keep healthy boundaries, not bully, and not be bullied. It shows up in an astonishing number of ways, with different terminations (cubic, rounded, octahedral) and blended with other materials, as in Apache Gold & Healers Gold (which I won't get into here).

IMAGE 120　　　　　　　　SOURCE

HEULANDITE floater crystal (India), more on page 175

The DNA of Crystals

IMAGE 38 octahedral **Pyrite cluster** page 42

Red Tiger Eye

How We Present Ourselves
(What the World Sees)

We can go two ways in our presentation to the world. Either we're pretending or showing a false self to the world (though it's not always intentional or manipulative) or we're 100% authentic and the same in all situations. I think it's unrealistic to expect us not to have a public persona, which may necessarily differ from our private one. This stone plays with that duality. It occurs naturally quite rarely, but just like our public persona, it's generally heat treated (as we are, by social pressures).

Scheelite, golden

Your Own Best Self
(Superego)

This is where your highest goals and personal standards live—it reflects and/or is the source of what you hope to achieve in the highest order. It informs your lesser self what your priorities and values are. It's quite impressive and rare stuff. Scheelite is naturally octahedral and dense, it hails from China. I've seen a striped blue, non-crystallizing version from Turkey, but I'm not sure it is truly a Scheelite.

IMAGE 39 octahedral **Scheelite** page 43

Super Seven, type 1

Hailing Multiple Sources

This is the traditional Super Seven. It's supposed to have seven key elements in it, which doesn't particularly matter to me. Visually, especially on cut pieces, you can see spindly strands of gold and purple and red (which are some of those elements). So long as it has that distinctive Super Seven look, I'm not counting whether it's a Super Three (with only three of the key elements) or a Super Four or a Super Seven. I think it's a beautiful occurrence. It is comparable vibrationally to Golden Rutilated Quartz. It's just dimensionally more sophisticated and complex. It is certainly one to spend more

SOURCE   IMAGE 121

LEMURIAN QUARTZ 3-sided point
(Brazil), more on page 74 + 175
The Mantle of Spiritual Governance

time with. I could have put it in Source, but preferred Self, because it's like our extraterrestrial origins, or connecting us to our alien allies.

IMAGE 40 **Super Seven** pendant page 44

Sunstone

Surprisingly hard to find, particularly in the rare, glittery Rainbow Lattice variety. It has that light play in common with Golden Rutilated Quartz and Tiger Eye, but chatoyancy can also be a Vision stone quality. I've associated it here with Self because of the color, but I haven't spent enough time with it to fully understand what its particular function might be.

Tiger Eye

See Me in Good Light
(Positive Reflection of the Self)

While Chrysocolla and Turquoise teach us how to be humble and go easy on ourselves, Tiger Eye teaches us how to appreciate and reflect on the best aspects of ourselves, our good qualities. In a group meditation, I picked Tiger Eye out and called it somebody's alter-ego, riding on a horse alongside them.

IMAGE 41 faceted **Tiger Eye** palm piece page 47

IMAGE 122   SOURCE

MERLINITE chunk (Madagascar), more on page 177
Develop your Wizardry

Example of Subgrouping the Stones of an Energy Zone

This is the only zone I'll be doing this with as an example for you. It's important to note that within each energy zone, the component stones can be matched into subgroups because of their common or related qualities.

I could fill out and demonstrate how I do this for all the energy zones, perhaps in future writings I will. I certainly have done this in my private classes already. Here's how my subcategorization works in the Heart zone.

While Heart is understandably about feeling, it can actually be split into three concept groups. The explicitly *feeling*-oriented Heart stones are: Malachite, Smoky Quartz, Milky Quartz, and Nephrite Jade. Malachite and Smoky Quartz are internally, personally oriented. Milky Quartz and Nephrite Jade work on us more from the outside in. You can read more about each below, in their individual listings.

The *love*-oriented Heart stones are Emerald, Rose Quartz, and Kunzite (you can read more about each below). Again, there's an orientation to each. The Emerald is deep within. The Rose Quartz is open to the world. Kunzite is particularly devoted to a higher love.

SOURCE   IMAGE 123

MOLDAVITE tektite (Besednice locality, Czech Republic), more on page 177

The Messages from On High

Lastly, the *community*-oriented Heart stones are Bloodstone, Lepidolite, and (not surprisingly) Relationship Stones. Relationship Stones capture groupings of people, whereas Lepidolite speaks to the intimate point of connection between them. Bloodstone reflects how we're blended into the larger society.

The reason these groupings are helpful, besides the way I've explained them thus far, is that if you're trying to help someone access their pent-up feelings (as you would with Malachite), a stone devoted to divine love (which Kunzite is about) would not be the first one you'd draw for. As you become familiar with each of the stone's qualities, it becomes possible to combine them meaningfully for yourself and with others.

✧ ✧ ✧

Bloodstone

I Am One among Many
(Self in Community)

I rarely have occasion to use Bloodstone,
but it's beautiful and there's nothing like it to represent us
(the red blobs, see image for reference) in the context of others
(the other red blobs) in the larger context of community (of
green). Sometimes, as we consider where we fit into the world, Bloodstone is just what we need. Likewise, it's good to bring into play if we're not fitting in or at odds with the world. In the Crystals for Life section, I speak of ascension stones, and how important our sense of obligation, or responsibility to the collective is. Although it's not an ascension stone per se, Bloodstone could certainly be considered as an often missing link in our personal quest for ascension, because of how it reflects our relationship to the whole of humanity. While most Bloodstones are red on a green background, there's a significant amount of it that has a blue background, which again gives us the opportunity (as with green and blue Fluorite) to consider whether we are more "green people" or "blue people."

IMAGE 42 large **Bloodstone** boulder page 48

IMAGE 124   SOURCE

NEBULITE aka Chrome Chalcedony nodule
(Turkey), more on page 178

Galactic Federations

Emerald

More than You Know
(Deeper Love)

Emerald is a wonderful, six-sided crystal that's more muted in color in lower quality stones (which I prefer). It's the stone that taught me not to clear and cleanse crystals because it lost all its energy when I did that to one I got over 30 years ago. It's possible to find tumbled or small chunks of Emerald relatively cheaply. Regrettably, most people selling raw crystals have drenched them in grease to give them a brighter (more marketable) color. I had vendors denying they were doing that, even as I was wiping my oily hands off. Frustrating. I don't know why people can't be honest about this sort of thing.

IMAGE 43 entwined **Emerald** crystals page 49

Jade, Nephrite

I am Here for You
(The Embrace of Mother Earth)

The soothing element of this stone comes directly from it representing Gaia or Mother Earth, which I help people visualize as the basin of the oceans and lakes, holding us the way it holds the waters. The continents themselves could be likened to Nephrite Jade. It is truly one of my favorites and my love for it is quite separate from its mythical status in Asia.

Originally, China's national stone was Nephrite Jade. Imperial fashions shifted and it was replaced by the more colorful Jadeite, from Burma. Jadeite is still preferred in Asia in general, particularly if it's neon emerald green, but I've heard China has reclaimed Nephrite as its national stone.

Most of the Nephrite in the world comes from Canada. There is some left in China, including the lesser known red and yellow varieties, and Siberia is known for its own particularly beautiful type of green Nephrite, and a gorgeous white variety.

IMAGE 44 **Nephrite Jade** tumbled palm piece page 50 and Buddha page 188

Kunzite

Embracing Spirit
(Higher Love)

This stone is how I see us connecting personally, emotionally, and with

SOURCE   IMAGE 125

NIRVANA QUARTZ (Zimbabwe), more on page 178

Ascended Multi-Dimensional Masters

love for our G8D or deities, spirits, and angels. It takes us high up, while keeping us connected to our heart. Many people have a fraught relationship with their religion. Kunzite can help them find their way back home, assuming that's a bond you want to re-establish. The key if it feels challenging, is to find what is pure and good about the belief system you once loved, or have more recently discovered, and connect with that.

Kunzite is actually the pink variety of Spodumene, of which there is also Hiddenite (green) and Triphane (yellowish green). These other types are far more obscure, but treasured by some. Nothing gets as much love as the pink Kunzite though, which hails from Brazil and Pakistan. What I'm looking for in a specimen of Kunzite is termination. It has a distinctive diagonal termination style, akin to the Naica Selenite. Looking at it from the side, it can be kind of pink. But when you look at it head on, through the termination, the color deepens dramatically to become almost fuchsia. Kunzite is also often etched.

IMAGE 45 palm sized **Kunzite** crystal page 51

Lepidolite

Connection with Family, Friend, and Foe
(True Intimacy)

Unusually, this purple stone does not hail from the higher energy zones, which purple generally suggests it might. It's a Heart stone that speaks to the contact point we have with other people, whether close to us or even our enemies. When polished, it can have a waxy surface, which feels a bit like human skin. That's part of why it ended up as a Heart stone and why it speaks to our connection with people, interestingly not only those we feel close or connected to warmly.

Lepidolite is mostly from Brazil. It can have botryoidal (bubbly) termination or appear in sheets. In one particularly rare occurrence, there are rhomboid (diamond-shaped) clear white (not purple) sections embedded in those purple sheets. I call this Diamond Lepidolite. It's also called bi-color in this case. And Lepidolite can come yellow too.

IMAGE 46 overlapping and standing **Lepidolite** hearts page 52

IMAGE 126   SOURCE

PYRITE CONCRETION infinity formation (China), more on page 180

Alignment of Beings in the Ground

Malachite

Get in Touch: What's Going on Inside
(Feelings)

Combining the black color of openness with the traditionally green color of the heart, I've found this to be a natural for opening the heart. Expressing our feelings can be hard and Malachite is here to help. The more black it has in it, the more dense, heavy, profound and grounding the sensation it offers. More valuable display pieces have elaborately swirling green patterns. Most Malachite on the market comes pretty exclusively from the Congo.

IMAGE 47 standing **Malachite** display or palm piece page 53

Milky Quartz

Compassion for One and All
(Nurturance)

A lot of Quartz is either milky or totally white, as are the super rough pieces you find in the woods in New England. It moves from Channel, where clear Quartz lives, to Heart because of this and takes on an important heart feeling function by representing compassion and nurturance. You can find Milky Quartz from wherever Quartz grows, the world over. A particularly sweet variety comes from Morocco, where there are pure Quartz geodes that get cracked open into matching halves. The glittery Milky Quartz within is hard to beat for beauty and purity. They used to be quite cheap and abundant, but I think that supply is waning.

IMAGE 48 large soft-cut **Milky Quartz** healing scanner page 54

SOURCE   IMAGE 127

DIAMOND SELENITE crystals (USA), more on page 180
Landed Space Station

Pink Tourmaline

Rose Tinted Glasses

This type of Tourmaline is similar to Kunzite, but not as high in vibration. In fact, it has a more personable, relatable aspect to it. It's almost like the loving kindness shown by G8D to us. Aside from the effective practicality of Black Tourmaline, Pink Tourmaline is my favorite. Often it's found growing in Milky Quartz, which is a nice combination, energetically.

Serpentine, Forest Jade variety

Forest Jade is the name I've given to this olive drab pseudo-Jade. It's not as soothing as Nephrite itself, but it's the closest in appearance to the real thing, among fakes. And it's not technically fake, as in manufactured, it's a real stone that simply resembles Nephrite Jade closely. Although not the exact same color, this is what is most often sold as being Jade out of Asia. If you ever see a huge boat or animal carved out of what is said to be Jade, it will more than likely have been crafted from this Serpentine variety. Ditto the ubiquitous "Jade" rollers and a host of other cut and polished items. It has black splotches, which are bigger and more irregular in shape than the black which shows up in true Nephrite.

IMAGE 49 large **Forest Jade** palm piece page 55

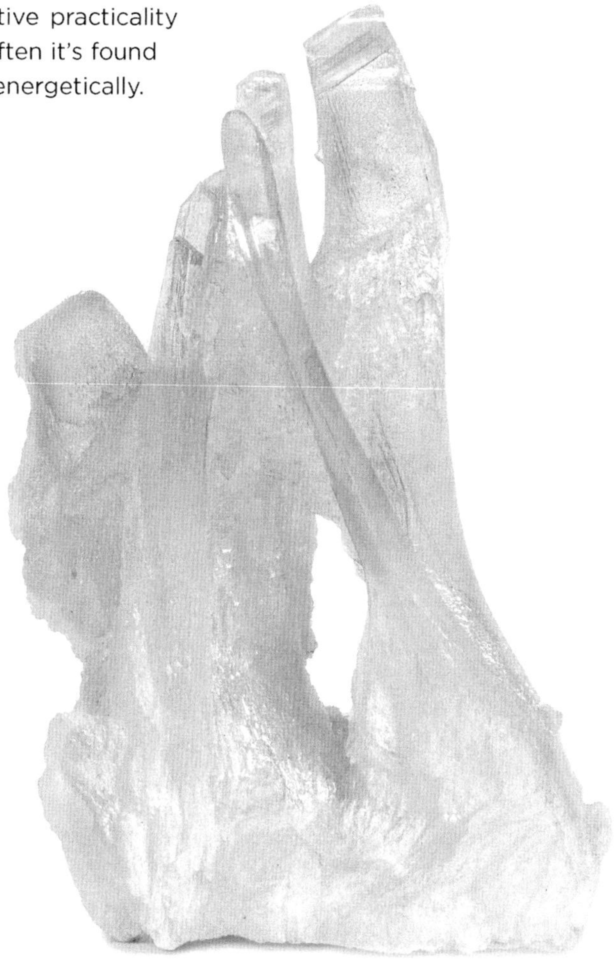

Serpentine, New Jade

Almost There

Also known as Water Jade or China Jade, this is a great low-budget Serpentine alternative to real Jade. Even though it can be a much softer light green, and it doesn't really look like Jadeite or Nephrite to the trained eye, it offers a comparably soothing Jade feeling for a fraction of the price. It's mostly cut

IMAGE 128   SOURCE

FLYING SELENITE cluster (Mexico), more on page 180

Reach for the Heavens

into rollers, freeform palm pieces, animals, and more. I've never seen it rough.

IMAGE 50 **New Jade** perfume bottle-form page 56

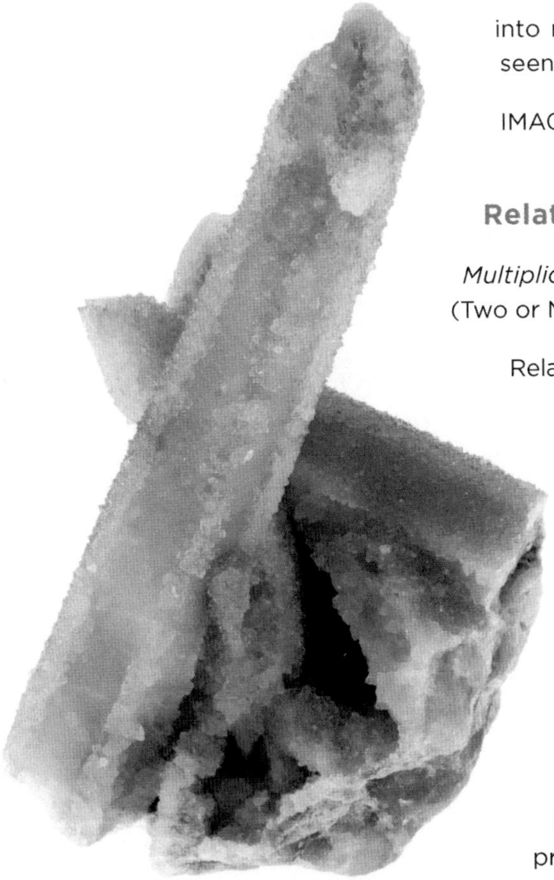

Relationship Stones

Multiplicity and Coexistence
(Two or More)

Relationship stones, including twins (pairs) and family stones (three or more conjoined points), are often Quartzes. They were portrayed in my card deck with a Lemurian tantric twin, which is two Lemurian points fused together. In general, Relationship Stones can have up to a handful of points before they become clusters. What they enable us to do is project our vision for a set of potential relationships: couples, parents, child(ren), etc. The people represented don't have to be related, pets could certainly be included.

IMAGE 17 **Red Cap Amethyst** twin points page 21

IMAGE 43 folded **Emerald** crystals page 49

IMAGE 51 **pink Madagascar Relationship Stone**, a twin (two primary stones) and family (with supporting crystals) that is also a **transmitter** page 57

IMAGE 63 triple termination standing **Candle Quartz** page 69

IMAGE 103 twin **Dark Amethyst** crystals page 110

SOURCE   IMAGE 129

SPIRIT QUARTZ transmitter (South Africa), more on page 181

Cosmic Wand

Rose Quartz

I Open My Heart to All Beings
(Unconditional Love)

While the concept of Rose Quartz—unconditional love—is very welcoming and attractive, it's not for everyone, at least not all the time. Few of us can open up that wide immediately. We need certain other steps to be taken to prepare us for this level of accessibility and openness. In a healing session, it's only used later, if the person feels safe and ready.

Rose Quartz originally came mostly from Brazil, but Madagascar has tons of it too, and both are comparable in their range of color and qualities. Generally, the more transparent, dark pink, and gemmy, the more valuable it will be. More milky and less pink is worth less. The U.S. has some quality Rose Quartz, but you rarely see it on the market.

IMAGE 52 large **Rose Quartz** sphere page 58 and palm piece 176

Smoky Quartz

Releasing Toxicity
(Forgiveness)

This type of Quartz became smoky in color due to its natural exposure to radioactivity in the ground. It transmuted that toxicity and rendered it harmless. I take this as a powerful metaphor for our own capacity to forgive and let go. I consider this to be an ideal stone (next to Shungite) for defense against EMFs and it's a softer, gentler stone to have around. I'm a big fan.

Smoky Quartz comes mostly from Brazil, with notable African sources, and a very wonderful occurrence out of New Hampshire in the United States. I find polished slightly more accessible, but a soft-surfaced point is also great. As mentioned elsewhere, you will rarely find a natural Smoky (or Citrine) cluster. And when it gets super saturated in the ground, becoming black, it's called a Morion Smoky (see the Channel energy zone for that one).

IMAGE 53 perfectly colored **Smoky Quartz** heart page 59

IMAGE 130   SOURCE
_____

BLUE/GREEN TOURMALINE ON SMOKY QUARTZ
crystal (Brazil), more on page 181

Crystallization of Intention

Tanzurine

This is a fancy name given to an Aventurine from Tanzania, whose green and cherry red varieties are nice and sparkly. The latter is (or possibly both are) apparently colored by Lepidolite inclusions. Although I like it, I haven't spent nearly enough time with it, energetically, to have it replace my more usual red and green go-to stones.

Unakite

Unakite combines a kind of pinkish orange with a muted green, both plausible heart colors. Beyond appreciating it aesthetically, I've only found use for it in jewelry.

Watermelon Tourmaline

A natural for the Heart zone, Watermelon Tourmaline has a red or green shell with the opposite inside, best seen as a cross section. The combination of these colors is appropriate but I've never worked with this material because it's so expensive and I'm happier with other green and red stones I've been able to find larger and more helpful. Stunning in jewelry though!

Zoisite

Zoisite is very close energetically to Emerald, what with its green background and black speckles. It's nice to find on its own but is mostly mined and prized when it has red Ruby splotches mixed in with it. Imagine an Emerald with added grounding value, and you have Ruby in Zoisite.

SOURCE   IMAGE 131

ORANGE ZINCITE crystallization (Poland), more on page 182

Vision or Inspiration in Source

Amazonite

I love the gentle healing energy of Amazonite, particularly if it's gemmy (mostly cut, from Brazil and Madagascar) or crystallized (from the U.S. and Pakistan).

Amber

(Easing Inflammation)
May This Burden Be Lifted

Originally, Eastern European Baltic Amber came from an extinct variety of 60-million-year-old pine trees that used to profusely leak sap all down their sides. It comes in various colors like butterscotch (whitish yellow), citrine (rich yellow), cherry (red), and even green (actually, a greenish yellow). Now you can find it from Mexico (the Chiapas material is particularly nice), and Colombia. Some types from Indonesia and the Dominican Republic turn blue with a black light.

Because it's so light, Amber seems to lift any blockage as if by magic. It's like osmosis, the energy goes from what's more dense and packed (like a tumor) toward what's free and light (like the Amber). I relieved a toothache by holding Amber to my cheek while driving. After that tooth was pulled, a Butterscotch Amber choker necklace was quite soothing.

One thing to avoid (or embrace if you like it, and the price is right) is Copal. It's very young or immature Amber (sometimes less than 10,000 years old) that hasn't yet fully fossilized. It's even lighter in density than real Amber and you can get bigger pieces of it for less money (from Madagascar and parts of Latin America). Just know that most vendors, including your local shops, are lying when they call it Amber.

IMAGE 54 **Mexican Chiapas Amber** freeform carving page 60

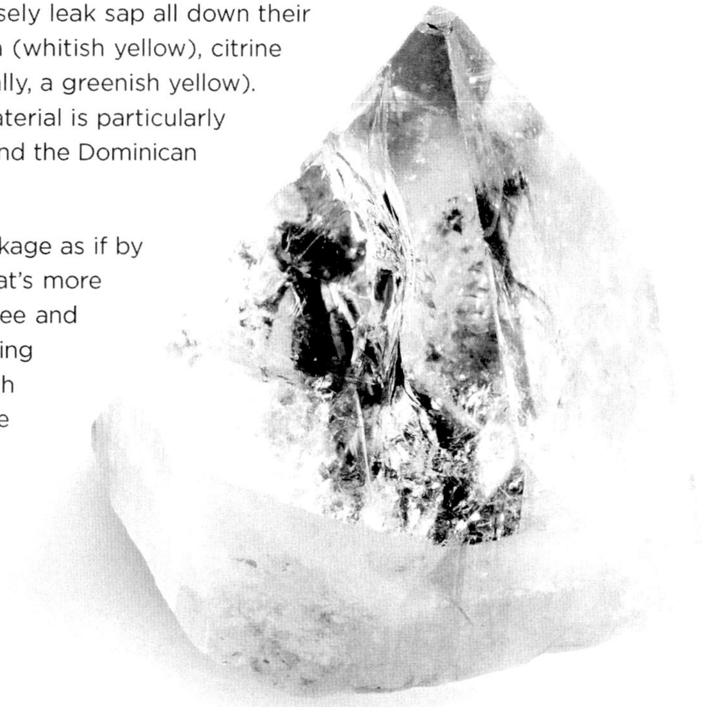

IMAGE 132   CHANNEL

APOPHYLLITE natural generator crystal (India), more on page 183

The Ascencion Stone

Amethyst Flower

Lasting Love

Found only in Brazil, Amethyst Flowers are circular crystal clusters that have fallen over each other, forming attractive and overlapping radial formations. Because it's not very purple and the shapes are not always harmonious, they're not as popular as they might be. Perhaps nobody's ascribed to them a big enough mantle, in terms of a healing superpower. I know that for me, I'll reach for a Milky Quartz, or either the Lavender, or Dark Amethyst varieties before using an Amethyst Flower. Still, aesthetically, they are beautiful and I definitely seek out perfect starbursts.

IMAGE 55 Brazilian starburst **Amethyst Flower** floater page 61

Amethyst, light

No World Cannot Be Healed
(Spiritual Cleansing)

I also call this Lavender Amethyst. I'm the only person I know of who makes a distinction between Dark Amethyst (see Vision) and Light or Lavender Amethyst, which is really quite wonderful. For people who want an Amethyst cluster to condition their session room or whatnot, I recommend this highly. Under a healing table is a nice idea because the gentle lavender mist will waft up from it, lending healing energy to all in its path.

An alternative with comparable function could also be a darker Amethyst cluster. I find Dark Amethyst most useful for Vision as a point or two, separated from the cluster. The cluster itself has this more generalized healing function. A rare and

CHANNEL   IMAGE 133

AURA QUARTZ cluster (China), more on page 60 + 183

The Disembodied Self

wonderful variety of Lavender Amethyst comes in the unusually elongated Amethyst points from Vera Cruz, Mexico. Some of these can have three sides to their point, and resemble Lemurian Quartzes. Having an elongated Amethyst (light or dark), which also happens in bigger chunky cathedralized points out of Bolivia, is a real gift.

IMAGE 56 small **Lavender Amethyst** cluster page 62

Anhydrite, blue

An Angel's Touch

When Anhydrite, affectionately called Angelite, is massive (i.e. not crystallized), it's a uniform baby blue, and comes from Peru. I like polished pieces, particularly with a matte (instead of high gloss) finish. I could have called it a Voice stone because it certainly speaks with a gentle voice. But its healing quality has been corroborated by me having worked with crystallized Blue Anhydrite (from Mexico), which forms into flaring fans or tight V's called Angel Wings. The idea is that they have the healing touch of an angel.

IMAGE 57 **Angel Wing Anhydrite** (or **Angelite**) page 63

IMAGE 134   CHANNEL

BLACK TOURMALINATED QUARTZ sphere (China), more on page 184

Compassionate Omnidirectional Boundaries

Aragonite, brown, non-crystallized

Healing from Inside

This material is an unsung hero. Sometimes, it grows attached to Rhodochrosite in Argentina. I've heard it called Rhodochrosite by at least one vendor, but it's really a kind of creamy brown calcium-rich Aragonite. Larger quantities with less vibe can be found in Morocco, but in either location it's got a great swirling and yummy brown layered pattern. Those large stone lamps from Mexico are often made with Aragonite too (if they're more flowy, soft-to-the-touch, and biological looking) versus Onyx (which is harder, glassier, and has a more Quartz-like vibe to it).

IMAGE 58 **Brown Aragonite** bowl page 64

Blue Lace Agate

Soothing Layers

All-around soothing, this light blue, layered Agate hails from Africa and is becoming more scarce. It's mostly sold in tumbled stones, though sometimes it appears in small, broken up, irregularly shaped geodes. Because it necessarily has layers, I like to think of it as working its magic on multiple levels of our being.

IMAGE 59 heart shaped **Blue Lace Agate** geode page 65

Cactus Quartz

Directed Healing

Cactus Quartz is distinctive because the crystals end with a little scepter-ish point. The rest of each crystal is bristling with smaller points. They can be more purple or yellow, but are not quite Citrines in the latter case, and the verdict is out as to whether they've been treated to get to that color. I consider Cactus Quartz to be comparable to Lavender Amethyst, particularly if it matches that color, and in terms of its function as a spiritual cleanser. It is because the points are more elongated that I consider it a bit more directional.

IMAGE 60 harmonious **Cactus Quartz** cluster page 66

Calcite, blue

Scoop of Peace

Another nice light blue stone, comes in tumbled form or as freeform display piece carvings, sometimes in rough chunks. Like many other Calcites, they get acid washed to get rid of the dustiness, seal up the surface, and make them pleasantly soft to the touch.

IMAGE 166 **Blue Calcite bowl** page 175

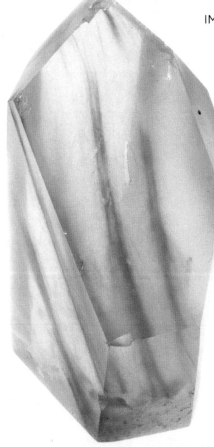

CHANNEL   IMAGE 135

BLUE TARA QUARTZ generator (Brazil), more on page 185

Channel Vision

Calcite, Honey or Golden Healer

Healing Sunset

Golden Healer Calcite, also called Honey Calcite, is the fancy New Age name for what is otherwise (when in small chunks or tumbled) a fairly humble material. When you get a well-formed crystal of Calcite in this color, you get to experience its true majesty. Like all the Calcites, it has a gentle healing energy and the texture of the surface on these crystals is particularly nice to the touch (and eye).

IMAGE 61 **Golden Healer Honey Calcite** crystal on matrix page 67

Calcite, milky

May I Be Renewed
(Purification)

Milky Calcite is a softer and more forgiving version of Milky Quartz, good for recovery from physical trauma and located also in the Healing zone (as opposed to Milky Quartz, which represents compassion in the Heart zone).

IMAGE 62 **Milky Candle Calcite** cluster page 68

IMAGE 136   CHANNEL

ENTITY STONES (various sources), more on page 185

Embodiment by Spirit

Candle Quartz

Compassionate Healing

These are so named because they look like a melted candle stick, with cathedral-type terminations crawling up their sides. They're never clear and, as Milky Quartzes, they have to do with compassion and nurturance. I've also seen them called Pineapple Quartz.

IMAGE 63 triple pointed **Candle Quartz** page 69

CHANNEL   IMAGE 137

FAIRY STONE CONCRETIONS
(Canada), more on page 186

Adaptive Transformation

Celestite, blue

Heavenly Gifts
(Gratitude)

When I describe the energy of Celestite, also once called Celestine (like the prophecy), I explain that it's like water evaporating up to the sky, which then condenses and comes down again as rain. The light and dark blue of Celestite is admittedly celestial, but it's contrasted by the weight and density, both of the crystals themselves and the sandy and crumbly cement-like matrix they grow in. This combination of opposites, and the movement from above to below, symbolizes the raining down of blessings from heaven (which I also call heavenly blessings or mercies).

The reason I associate this stone with gratitude is because just like the rain, it falls when it falls. There's nothing you can do to make it happen and so it symbolizes things we get or are gifted, just for being us (without having to earn it).

IMAGE 64 **Celestite** cluster page 70

Chalcedony, indigo

Setting the Healing Standard

Because it's not translucent (like Indigo Fluorite) Indigo Chalcedony is lower on the energetic totem pole. Not to place values on different energy zones, they are all equal. Notice, there are no translucent stones in Root or Foundation, yet many in both Source and Channel are. In this case, the Indigo Chalcedony is darker than the Lavender Chalcedony and its vibration is more purple than soft blue. Before Lavender Chalcedony came on the market, Indigo Chalcedony was my go-to stone for calming, soothing, and realignment.

IMAGE 65 **Indigo Chalcedony** wafer page 71

Chalcedony, lavender

Restored Alignment

Lavender Chalcedony has become quite the rage in the past five+ years, since it was discovered in quantity in Turkey. Now I understand they'll have to dig down several miles to find more, and although my suppliers claim it's going to be harder to find, I'm not yet convinced of that. It's wonderful stuff, but because of its uniformity of color it's prized in China and all the material is bought for and polished there. It's not as cheap as it might be, but well worth it because there's almost no other stone that says realignment and general healing like this one.

IMAGE 66 **Lavender Chalcedony** palm sized cabochon page 72

Chalcedony, pink

Personal Care

Chalcedonies are creamy, uniformly colored Quartzes that never crystallize. They can be found in Turkey and as nodules in the Himalayas. Also, they exist most rarely as a pink Petrified Wood. While the Lavender Chalcedony is a perfect all-around healing stone, the Pink Chalcedony brings a softer, more loving aspect to the process that is more personal.

IMAGE 67 standing **Pink Chalcedony Petrified Wood** page 73

IMAGE 138   CHANNEL

IRRADIATED QUARTZ point (Arkansas), more on page 187

The Attack Dog

Chevron Amethyst

Mindful Stewardship
(Charity)

I used to have this stone in Heart (for my card deck) but have moved it to Healing. What I like about Chevron Amethyst is that it features alternating layers of purple (spiritual mission) and white Quartz (compassion). The combination of spirituality and compassion is ultimately charity, an important part of Tikkun Olam, or healing/repairing the world (in Hebrew).

IMAGE 68 rough **Chevron Amethyst** crystal page 74

CHANNEL   IMAGE 139

BLACK KYANITE fan crystal (Brazil), more on page 187
The Psychic Sweeper

Chrysoprase

Chrysoprase is wonderful in jewelry and occasionally very similar to Prehnite energetically, but not quite as healing. Still, some people love it. I tend to have my favorites, when it comes to green and blue stones, but Chrysoprase is certainly one of the greats. It combines both colors, and is from Australia and China. It also has more Quartz in it, making it harder than Prehnite, which has more Calcite in it.

Cintamani Stone

Ancient Healing

The word Cintamani is Hindu, and it's analogous to the Philosopher's Stone in Western lore. Some think of it as a Tektite, like Moldavite—but because of its layering, I believe it's a weathered Obsidian—originally some sort of molten glass. I like it because of its rich texturing, weathered tiers, and its pock-marked craters. If you shine a light through it, it's a gentle smoky color like an Apache Tear or even a Smoky Quartz. This is definitely a vibrational power house, though perhaps not to the extent of the hype around it. For example, it's also called Agni Manitite, based on the ancient Sanskrit term agni mani, which means "Pearl of the Divine Fire." It was, after all, born of a molten past!

A similar material called Saffordite looks even more like a round Tektite—and might actually be one. It's from Arizona and found in both small sizes and small quantities. And it's also called Cintamani stone, perhaps because of its resemblance to the Indonesian material described above. It may also be an Obsidian.

IMAGE 69 large Indonesian **Cintamani stone** page 75

Cobalto Calcite

Physical Heart Healing

Gorgeous ranges of pink—these come less impressively from Congo, where they're like a sheet of colored sandpaper on matrix—and more pleasantly (and increasingly expensively) from Morocco, where they can have rounded or more unusually spiky terminations. I consider this material similar to Pink Fluorite in that it's a heart healer, designed to help mend the broken heart, but perhaps more physically (being a Calcite).

IMAGE 70 standing pink **Cobalto Calcite** on matrix page 76

Danburite

Receiving Higher Love

Combines the qualities of Topaz (the Body Whisperer, by which we talk inwardly to our bodies) and Kunzite (the Higher Love stone), for a very interesting blend of body connectedness and the embrace of spirit. I channeled the phrase "Receiving Higher Love" because I think of it as facilitating our capacity to synthesize the affections of the Divine. Pretty elevated stuff!

IMAGE 71 unusual, full cluster of **pink Danburite** page 77

Fluorite, lavender

Calm Your Nerves
(Relaxant)

More purple than blue, this type of Fluorite is difficult to

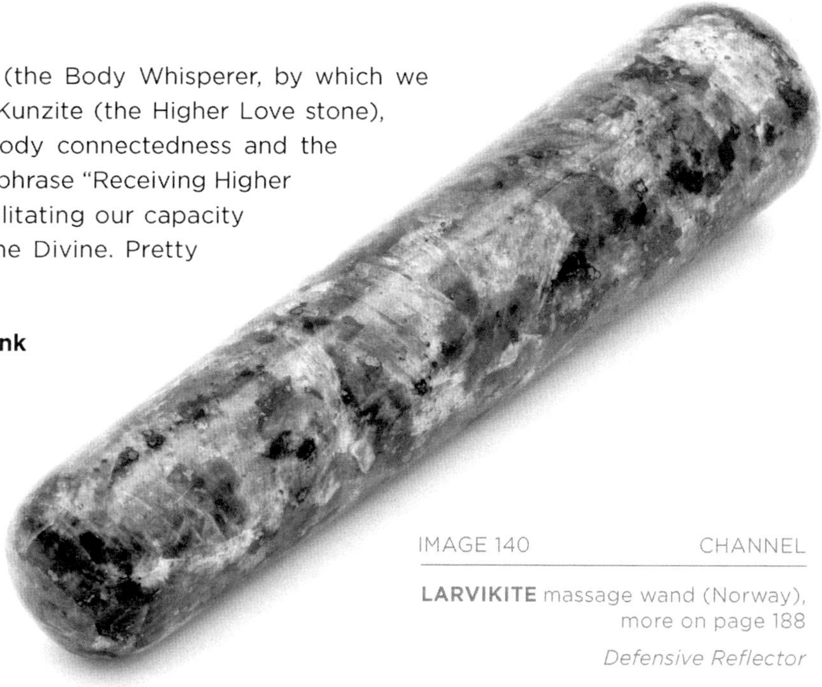

IMAGE 140   CHANNEL

LARVIKITE massage wand (Norway), more on page 188

Defensive Reflector

find. I've discovered only eggs and a Buddha (and a few standing freeform display pieces) in this material. Less of a re-aligner than the Lavender Chalcedony, Lavender Fluorite is a very fast emotional soother.

IMAGE 72 **Lavender Fluorite** palm-piece egg page 78

Fluorite, pink

Spiritual Heart Healing

This is the second type of Fluorite that finds itself in the Healing energy zone. It is for healing the broken heart. Added value for me is that it comes in my favorite crystallization, octahedral, so it's covered in pyramids.

CHANNEL   IMAGE 141

MOONSTONE multi-tone (India), more on page 188
Full Chakra Filter

IMAGE 73 octahedral Mexican **Pink Fluorite** cluster page 79

Hanksite

This is a mysterious stone, both a Sulfate (based on Sulfur) and a Carbonate (based on Carbon), which is soluble (which means it can be dissolved) in water. It looks like a double terminated, waxy, and porous Quartz, literally the same crystal structure. I really like it. I think of it as the kind of blending of a Quartz battery crystal and a healing Milky Calcite.

Hemimorphite

An interesting blue stone from China that resembles blue Aragonite and also Gem Silica. It's unusual and can fetch higher prices but has not shown itself to be particularly distinctive or better at any particular function than any other blue stone I already work with more commonly.

Herkimer Diamond

The Impenetrable Fortress
(Health and Strength)

People unfamiliar with these can't believe they haven't been faceted. They are naturally double terminated and unique formations of Quartz from near Herkimer, New York. Very alike (but still distinguishable to the trained eye) are similarly shaped crystals from Pakistan and Morocco. Herkimer Diamonds often form in groupings, connected naturally but broken apart in mining (so they get glued back together). When it's ultra-clear, this crystal is highly prized, but I prefer bigger, imperfect pieces that are palm sized. They often have rainbows and may be skeletal (which I explain a bit later).

Energetically, it feels to me like the tightest formation of Quartz, hence my referring to it as the impenetrable fortress having to do with health and strength.

IMAGE 74 semi-tabular **Herkimer Diamond Quartz** page 80

IMAGE 142   CHANNEL

MORION SMOKY QUARTZ crystal
(USA), more on page 189
The Guardian Watcher

Jade, Jadeite

Jadeite is the other variety of true Jade, additional to Nephrite, which I discuss in Heart. Guatemalan Blue Jadeite, featured in Voice, is pretty recognizable (but somewhat of a different animal). In this section here, I'd like to talk mostly about Burmese Jadeite, which is the primary and most desirable type of Jade in Asia. It's harder to identify, just by looking at it. I like to think the real stuff resembles a petrified gel or body wash. But I don't hesitate to get it appraised professionally when it matters (i.e. when larger amounts of money are being spent), because there are similar looking stones like Serpentine and Bowenite that are rampantly sold as Jadeite. Treatments can also make more dissimilar stones resemble and be sold as Jadeite. Jadeite naturally ranges from white to darker colorful tones and can feature splotches of lavender (my favorite) or dark green. The bright lighter green Imperial Jade is the most prized, commercially.

Vibrationally, and because of all of these differences, Jadeites could fairly be attributed to several different energy zones. Because it's not easily identifiable and rarely is available in palm size or larger, I've shied away from working with it metaphysically. There is of course a huge amount of existing lore surrounding Jadeite, but with the relative abundance and more palpable energy from Nephrite and its facsimiles like New Jade, I mostly just go with them. I've put Jadeite into the Healing energy Zone because I believe that the true white Jadeite is like a deluxe and more soothing version of Milky Quartz, and I appreciate it for the same purposes, having to do with nourishment and compassion (as well as possibly purity).

Jade, Siberian white Nephrite

Above I discussed white Jadeite. There's another white Jade, but it's a Nephrite, and it comes from Siberia. Although the more purely colored it is, the more valued it's been by the market, I prefer when it has honey toned discolorations, even looking toasted or blackened. This takes it away from notions of purity and compassion, but it seems to make it more nourishing. Strongly recommended, if you can get a hold of it.

Jet

Let Go of What No Longer Serves
(Internal Clearing)

This is an odd petrification of wood that doesn't get replaced with Quartz, so it's not heavy. In fact, it's actually about as light as Amber. It has a similar function, to remove impurities and blockages, but it does so within us. It's like your personal psychic, emotional, and physical Roomba. I believe the best material I've gotten comes from UK and Poland. I also believe that coal has been sold as Jet out of China.

IMAGE 75 palm-sized chunk of **Jet** page 81

Larimar

Healing through the Waters

CHANNEL   IMAGE 143

NUUMITE tumbler, more on page 189
Cosmic Deflector

A giant among stones, it's hugely popular—both expensive and plentiful—out of the Dominican Republic. Mostly cut into jewelry, the better-quality stuff is more pleasing to look at. Energetically, I haven't spent much time with it, but I certainly appreciate it as a healing stone. It's an example of a stone in one zone that is relevant to another. I consider it the Voice Healer.

Also called Pectolite or Dolphin Stone—as well as the blue stone of Atlantis—I feel like I can hear it better under water. I'd recommend pairing it with Aquamarine Fluorite.

IMAGE 76 natural chunk of **Larimar** (with a polished face) page 82

Lingam Stone

Opposites Come to Rest
(Equilibrium)

In the section on crystal shapes, I talk about how the egg is emergent on one side. These are emergent on both sides. The mythology around them in India has them representing the male sex organ, which is paired with the female Yoni for ritual. I have a different take, not thinking of it in terms of gender at all and not thinking of it vertically. I think of the Lingam Stones as best placed horizontally, where they can impart balance and equilibrium. Originally these were said to be formed this way in rivers, but I think they are all formed by hand or machine, nowadays.

IMAGE 77 **Lingam Stone** with an unusual color and pattern page 83

Lithium Quartz

There's Got to Be a Better Way
(Healing the Broken Mind)

Lithium is a medication but here in this soft purplish pink incarnation, it's just calming to the mind, reintegrating, and seemingly offering another alternative for mending the mind.

IMAGE 78 **Lithium Quartz** point, also an angel phantom page 84

IMAGE 144   CHANNEL

BLACK OBSIDIAN chunk (Mexico), more on page 189
The Open Space of Possibility

Mangano Calcite

This is a wonderful variety of Calcite that you can get cut in a lighter, massive, or uncrystallized variety, and also find in various shades of gently translucent pink in the more valuable crystal form from China. It's pretty highly prized and the shape of these crystals is nice, expanding like a fan up to an arcing termination.

Moon Quartz

Healing our Vision

I've chosen Moon Quartz—an unusual occurrence out of Arizona, mostly of smaller and tumbled stones—to be a vision Healing stone, meaning it's designed to help us recover our capacity to envision. It's a lot like a Moonstone, but it has a more healing, rather than an imaginative agenda.

CHANNEL   IMAGE 145

GOLDEN SHEEN OBSIDIAN sphere (Mexico), more on page 69 + 190
Light in the Darkness

IMAGE 79 tumbled **Moon Quartz** page 85

Obsidian, Apache Tear

Apache Tear Obsidian is essentially Smoky Obsidian. If it's thin enough you can see its smoky translucence. This volcanic glass was thrown up from eruptions and hardened into little balls coated with white ash before landing again. Very wonderful stuff, similar to Smoky in that it can relieve you of some of your sorrow. It also represents a graceful recovery from volcanic transformation.

Obsidian, Midnight Lace

Healing through the Layers

Midnight Lace Obsidian has wispy bands of darker smoky lines running through it. I consider it comparable to Smoky Quartz and Apache Tear Obsidian. It makes for striking pieces of jewelry.

IMAGE 80 **Midnight Lace Obsidian** pendant page 86

Onyx, black

Black Onyx is like a much darker version of Red Jasper, very balancing, but more mysterious because of its obscurity. Onyx also comes in other colors that can be richly patterned, getting it confused with Aragonite and Alabaster. When it's lighter, Onyx also lends itself to being dyed.

Opal, pink

Found primarily in Peru, to my knowledge, Pink Opal has a soft energy but not quite as soft or healing as Pink Chalcedony.

Opal, white or Australian

Holding Fast

For some reason, very early in the game (around 1990), I picked up on white Opal as being very strong (almost like a black hole, but white), pulling matter into it in a strangely fortifying way. That's a pretty complex dynamic to explain or comprehend, so forgive me for even attempting. I'll add or qualify that I'm talking about Opals that are not super color-ful, maybe even lower quality pieces (including more light and monochromatic versions from Ethiopia). Boulder Opal, which is Opal-in-matrix featuring colorful fissures where true Opal has settled, is a good example of what I'm driving at energetically. Maybe it's that life energy has been trapped or captured, in this particular experience of Opal, for you to access and harness.

IMAGE 81 see a **Boulder Opal** horse head page 87

IMAGE 146   CHANNEL

CLEAR QUARTZ natural Lemurian generator (Colombia), more on page 73 + 191

Clarity and Focus

Petalite

I've only ever seen this tumbled, it's one of the ones I held off on for years, till I got the right source. It's a lot like Rainbow Moonstone, but more Milky. I consider it belonging here in the Healing energy zone.

Pink Amethyst

Also known as Pink Quartz, this is wonderful stuff from Patagonia in Argentina. A relatively recent find, a lot of it has hit the market for variable prices. Truly, it's a Pink Quartz (doesn't really look like Amethyst) and looks a lot like how you would think Rose Quartz would terminate (except that Rose Quartz looks totally different when it terminates, much smaller and more glassy). The points are not as stubby as Amethyst, but they are well defined and occur in geodes, which can be fragile. Finding a good specimen with good color in an intact geode is no easy feat. Consider it Pink Crystallizing Quartz meets Calcite. It definitely has a waxy Calcite feeling to it. Energetically, I would call it another heart healer, like Pink Fluorite and Cobalto Calcite.

Pink Halite

Wonderful stuff, it comes from a lake in California and apparently requires quite a muddy process to dig up. Once out and clean though, it's a wonder to behold, but a bit too fragile for my liking.

Prehnite, green

Soothing the Skin
(The Stone Aloe Vera)

I'm a big fan of Prehnite, it's usually polished and botryoidal (bubbly) with darker Tourmaline-looking Epidote crystals embedded in it. It really feels like a stone version of aloe vera and is particularly healing to the body surfaces, particularly the skin. Though just like an aloe vera drink, I wouldn't discount its capacity to favorably impact organs deeper within, through the skin.

IMAGE 82 cascading botryoidal cluster of **Prehnite** page 88

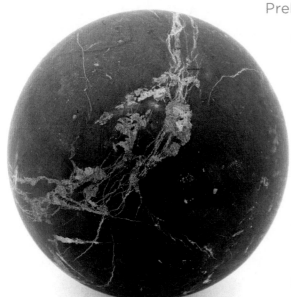

CHANNEL   IMAGE 147

SHUNGITE sphere with Pyrite (Russia), more on page 69 + 191
The Filtering Stone

Scolecite

Be Cleansed by the White Ash
(Extreme Purification)

While this appears in exquisite (and fragile) crystals out of India, I prefer it cut and polished, which reveals a wonderful chatoyant (shimmering in the light) patterning. It is a type of white that is not soft and soothing like Milky Quartz and Calcite. It's a much harder white, like the white ash of a fire, and has a cauterizing, purifying energy to it. It also reminds me of the white African judicial society masks of the Fang tribe in Gabon. Sometimes, ideally, justice can be cleansing.

IMAGE 148   CHANNEL

BLACK TEKTITE (Thailand),
more on page 192

Own your Aura

Selenite, Naica

Clearly Sealing

Have you seen the crystal cave pictures and videos from deep underground in Mexico? That's Naica and the Selenite there is superior to the more garden variety (plentiful, all pretty much the same) logs from Morocco. Two things make Naica Selenite special. It's often clear and also it has a beautiful angled termination, like Kunzite. I call that edge, like a clothing steam iron, a psychic sealer. It's optimum for closing wounds, physical or otherwise.

IMAGE 83 angled **Naica Selenite** sealer crystal page 89

Serpentine, Healerite

Rebirthing

Similar to New Jade, the Healerite variety of Serpentine, also known as Olive Serpentine, is actually healing and soothing (but not like Prehnite). I consider it regenerative, like spring, rather than in a fleshy sense (like Rhodochrosite).

IMAGE 84 **Healerite Serpentine** chunk page 90

Skeletal Quartz

Not All Is Lost, Hope
(Weakness in Strength)

Also known as Fenster Quartz, Skeletal Quartz is very similar to Herkimer Diamonds, which can also be skeletal. My favorites are either the Herkimer Skeletals or an old find from under the desert in Mexico (of which I have several pieces still). The structure of the stone is firm and solid, but it's broken up inside with lots of visible lines and air seemingly getting in. What's powerful about these is how strong they are, despite their compromised interior. They give us hope that we too can be strong, in spite of our infirmities.

IMAGE 85 **Skeletal Quartz** from Mexico page 91

Snowy & Mystic Healing Carnelian

Absorb the Static
(Bring into Alignment)

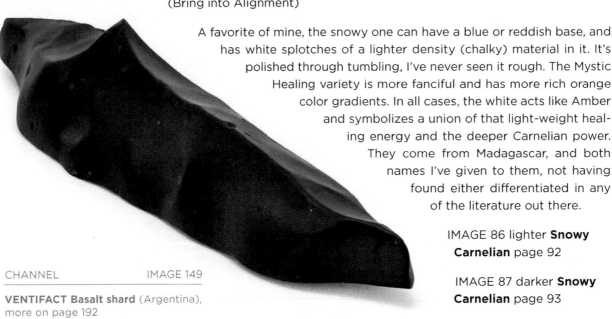

A favorite of mine, the snowy one can have a blue or reddish base, and has white splotches of a lighter density (chalky) material in it. It's polished through tumbling, I've never seen it rough. The Mystic Healing variety is more fanciful and has more rich orange color gradients. In all cases, the white acts like Amber and symbolizes a union of that light-weight healing energy and the deeper Carnelian power. They come from Madagascar, and both names I've given to them, not having found either differentiated in any of the literature out there.

IMAGE 86 lighter **Snowy Carnelian** page 92

IMAGE 87 darker **Snowy Carnelian** page 93

CHANNEL   IMAGE 149

VENTIFACT Basalt shard (Argentina), more on page 192
Clearing the Pathway

Stichtite

Very low density, almost chalky like Talc in texture, Stichtite is apparently hard to find remotely in Siberia. It resembles Sugilite, but because of its much softer feel and lighter density, feels better as a healing stone to me, rather than a Source or Vision stone (like Sugilite and Dark Purple Amethyst).

Stilbite, peach

This is a very beautiful crystal—whose unfortunate name is actually from the Greek—to shine or reflect. It's one of the Zeolites out of India. Zeolites are an eclectic group of minerals that are somehow related, but don't actually have much in common energetically. Stilbite often forms with Apophyllite but is never translucent. Stilbite has a cauliflower type of termination (also forming oddly into bow ties). I consider it a belly healing stone, in the way that Pink Fluorite is healing to the heart.

Water Quartz

Wash it Away

These were probably discarded broken crystals of Quartz that someone thought to tumble. They maintain some of their jagged edges, are not all rounded like traditionally tumbled stones, and never look like actual crystals. But they're soft everywhere and wouldn't cut you. Instead, they look like crystallized water and feel that way as well, like a flowing brook you put into your hands. Very good for washing away the unwanted.

IMAGE 88 **Water Quartz** nugget
page 94

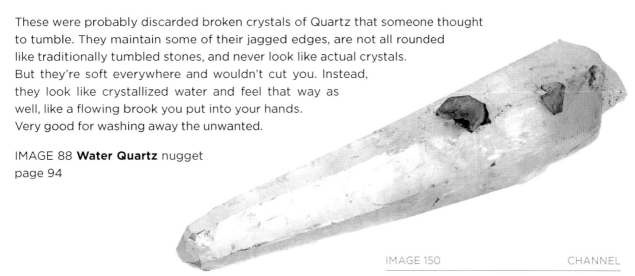

IMAGE 150   CHANNEL

DIAMANTINA LASER QUARTZ point (Brazil),
more on page 185

Nature's Wand

Aquamarine

Speaking to the Mind
(Upwards Communication)

I personally prefer and use Topaz, the Body Whisperer—for projecting my consciousness downward to listen to my body—rather than Aquamarine, which does the opposite. Aquamarine speaks upwardly from the body to the mind, the higher mind specifically. I usually go straight up to the higher heights with the Source-and-Channel-based ascension stones, but I think I would benefit from spending more time with Aquamarine. One thing I have determined is that Aquamarine is sort of the intellectual's stone, and as such I've dubbed it "the writer's stone" as well.

It's actually hard to find great Aquamarines to work with. They either come in low grade opaque tumblers (some nicer ones I've put into pendants) or as a quality terminated crystal for thousands of dollars. In spite of there being several dealers with Aquamarine at the show I did in Tucson this year, I found not a single piece that wasn't damaged or otherwise forgettable. I had searched for years to find one I was happy with. I've held it in my collection 'til just now. I'm releasing it back into my for-sale stock. Perhaps someone else can put it to better use than me. It's light blue and from Pakistan. But I'm keeping my dark blue Vietnamese Aqua.

IMAGE 89 dark blue **Veitnamese Aquamarine** page 95

CHANNEL   IMAGE 151

BLACK TOURMALINE double terminated standing batter crystal (China), more on page 57 + 184

Borders and Limits

Barite (blue, clear, green, and brown)

I'm a big fan of Barite. It comes in several colors, my favorite being blue and my second favorite being brown. The brown is a cross between Topaz and Smoky Quartz, which is a very intriguing internal voice stone to use. The blue is like Aquamarine, but more grounded in the body due to its weight, which makes it somehow related to Celestite.

Blue Quartz, uncrystallized

I like Blue Quartz. The prettiest material comes from Bahia, Brazil. It gets cut into everything from display pieces to cabochons. But there is some found in the U.S. too, mostly just rough, which is pretty nice too. I haven't really spent time with it, energetically, because I have other blue stones I prefer right here in this same energy zone.

IMAGE 169 **Brazilian Blue Quartz** generator page 178

Chrysocolla

Do unto Others As You Would Do to You
(Humility, Social Graces)

Chrysocolla is an extraordinary stone because it speaks both to our relationship with others and to our relationship with ourselves. Both require care and respect. Primarily from Peru, it occurs in a range of blues and greens due to its Turquoise and Malachite content. It can also be found from the Congo.

IMAGE 90 **Peruvian Chrysocolla** egg page 96

Gem Silica

Words Need Not Apply
(Spirit Communication)

Gem Silica is basically a high grade Chrysocolla featuring fine blue druzy Quartz on it. It's rare and wonderful and I've associated it with a high level of communication. On one level, it could be our communication with them (the spirits), but on another, it's more about their communication with each other.

IMAGE 152   CHANNEL

FADEN QUARTZ cluster (Pakistan),
more on page 58 + 186
Surviving the Interstitial Spaces

Girasol Quartz

Making Peace with the Unknown and the Unknowable
(Trust and Faith)

I've always loved this stuff, also known as Foggy Quartz. It's not Clear or Rose Quartz, it's opaque. You cannot see through it or, what you see is obscured. Because of that, I've associated it with our capacity to come to terms with the fact that we cannot always know outcomes. Being optimistic despite that demonstrates both faith and trust.

IMAGE 91 V-shaped **Girasol** (or **Foggy**) **Quartz** page 97

Jade, blue Jadeite

Honesty
(Truth)

Particularly from Guatemala, this material is like truth serum. You cannot lie with it in your system. That aspect of tapping into your authenticity and expressing it makes this a Voice stone. It's interesting to note that other Jades, like Nephrite, are Heart or Healing stones. They're an all-star team. Related, but not quite the same in energy, is the California Vonsen Blue Jade, which is apparently also called Dianite (named after Princess Diana) when it comes from Russia.

IMAGE 92 **Guatemalan Blue Jadeite** page 98

IMAGE 93 **California Vonsen Jade** page 99

Kyanite, blue

The Grounded Voice

My favorite form of Blue Kyanite is when it gets polished to hold or put into jewelry. When it's rough, it's often too chafey for me, which makes it feel like it dissipates (and makes less accessible) its energy. Once polished, I can get more into it and it feels more solid and weighty. Although I don't tend to use it in meditations or treatments because I have other blue stones I prefer, people swear by it (and its more unusual green and orange varieties).

IMAGE 94 gemmy **Blue Kyanite** cluster page 100

Lapis

I Say and Do What I Mean and Desire
(Finding Your Voice)

I call Lapis the axle or axis of the Voice energy zone. It's dominant! That doesn't mean the others aren't important too, it just means this one gets noticed first. It expresses both the process by which we discover

SOURCE   IMAGE 153

BLUE CRYSTALLIZED QUARTZ starburst floater (China), more on page 59 + 172
Frozen Flow

what we want to say in the world and the process by which we say it in order to get what we want and need out of the world.

I rarely see Lapis from Chile anymore, it went into jewelry exclusively. All of what I've seen comes from Afghanistan. The white that runs through it is Calcite, the gold is Pyrite, and the blue is Lazurite (which can crystallize nicely on its own). Lapis is always massive, not crystallized, and can range in color from deep dark blue to light blue (the less usual Denim Lapis variety). Too much Calcite in it, and not enough Pyrite, can make it kind of bland, energetically. You can tell if it's been dyed because the Calcite is light blue. And yet, I've had dealers break pieces in front of me to prove that the color inside is the same as the color outside (and that their material was not dyed).

IMAGE 95 richest **Lapis** color available (supposedly from the legendary old Mine 4) page 101

Lazulite

The Measured Tone

Lazulite is easy to confuse with Lazurite because their names are so similar. But it's different in that it's got spots of blue color in its massive form, rather than forming into crystals, and it's not what makes Lapis blue. I have not spent much time with it, but I liken it to Blue uncrystallized Quartz and have kept it around for a rainy day.

IMAGE 96 **Lazulite** chunk page 102

Lazurite

Lazurite is the blue coloring agent in Lapis, necessarily different from Lazulite. When it does crystallize, it's kind of a miracle because it's like the culmination or ultimate expression of that powerful blue in Lapis. I keep a piece in my collection and if they were more common, I'd recommend folks work with them energetically.

Prehnite, blue

I like Blue Prehnite almost as much as I like the green, it's just hard to find good pieces of it. It's also not quite as unique or powerful as Topaz, but it's similar enough to be a good companion or substitute for it.

IMAGE 154   SOURCE

BETA QUARTZ natural crystal (China), more on page 59 + 171

Multi-Dimensional Balance of Opposites

TRANSMITTER QUARTZ also a double terminated floater (Brazil), more on page 57 + 59

Sending & Receiving Intention

Richterite

Mostly, Richterite is found as the blue in Sugilite, but occasionally you can see it separated out. I have a good-sized pendant and a beaded necklace made exclusively from it. It's quite different from Lapis, more akin to Sapphire, but still closer to Sugilite. It's pretty high-level stuff, though I haven't put into words yet what it's all about. What I will say is that it has an upward pulling energy, in a complementary way to how Sugilite has a downward pulling energy.

Sapphire, blue

Sapphire is basically a blue Ruby and if the color's right (it has a range of colors itself) it'll knock your socks off. I pair it with Richterite, though it is more gemmy (when facet grade). It's certainly more grounding than Richterite and yet rather sublime. I know these things seem contradictory, but as I've mentioned before, energy zones can have their own distinct chakra systems within them, such that Voice can have its very own grounding stone. Sapphire appears to be that—a grounding force connected to Voice, but also from and connected to a very high place.

Sugilite

Bringing Vision into Being
(Spiritual Manifestation)

Pronounced with a hard G, like go, because of its discoverer being a Japanese gentleman with the last name of Sugi. I used to have Sugilite as a Source stone. I feel like I've demoted it by "lowering it" to Voice, but truly it speaks to the essential function of the voice to take the unmanifest, the unseen, and then to make it manifest and expressed in the real world. I call it the Manifestation Stone and rely on it for inspiration when I'm trying to make things happen in the world, particularly professionally.

In look and feel, besides being purple (which brings in that higher element), Sugilite is very similar to Lapis, although its range of actual content includes a much wider spectrum of mineral components. Most of what we have for Sugilite was mined in the 1970's and 1980's, after which mining for Manganese killed the search for Sugilite, as the process of mining Manganese overlooks (and possibly destroys) Sugilite.

The Chinese are in love with it still, specifically the pink gel variety which they use for jewelry and fine carvings. Americans have not quite caught up in either interest or investment in Sugilite, but I have stock-piled it because there really isn't much of great quality out there. I have many videos about it—where I explain the difference between lucent (light-penetrating) and chromatic (surface pattern-ing) Sugilite—as well as doing surveys of the wide range in possible gradations of it, from chalky and black to waxy and gel quality.

IMAGE 97 **Sugilite** chunk page 103 and dragon page 186

Topaz, clear

Calling All Cells
(The Body Whisperer)

When I want to get in touch with my body or send a wake-up call to all of its furthest reaches, I use Topaz. It's clear and watery but heavy and a good conductor, like the nervous system itself. My favorite is river worn Topaz. It and Nephrite seem to be among the only stones that are consistently river worn. If you see Blue Topaz, particularly in jewelry, it has generally been treated to arrive at that color. Blue Topaz starts to take on the energy signature of Aquamarine.

IMAGE 98 standing bluish **Clear Topaz** page 104

Turquoise

I am Good, I am Enough
(Self-Forgiveness)

IMAGE 156   SELF

SELF-HEALED CITRINE also a double terminated floater (Brazil), more on page 61 + 123

Making Myself Whole

This is perhaps the ultimate self-care stone. It's gentle, though not to a fault. It speaks to the care we have to take in managing our internal affairs. The tag phrases above say it all.

Like Jadeite, grading the different varieties of Turquoise is an art in itself, one I'm always open to learning much more about. There is a lot of fake Turquoise out there—mostly colored Howlite—and a big distinction is made between when it is stabilized for cutting or left natural (and still of a quality that lends itself to cutting). It comes from Mexico and Arizona, but also appears strangely from the Himalayas. It can be baby blue, dark blue, green, and with all types of variations. If it looks good and feels right, that might be your best method for choosing a Turquoise, as a non-professional.

IMAGE 99 **Mexican Turquoise** page 105

Agate, Patterned

Explore the Possibilities
(Creativity)

The easiest way to find Patterned Agate is in slabs that are put onto easel stands for display. They often come dyed, but the natural ones are still out there and are available in an astonishing selection of patterns. Pricing can range widely, from very cheap to surprisingly expensive. Ultimately, the cost reflects the complexity of the pattern or the value placed on it by the seller.

IMAGE 100 large **Pattern Agate** slab pag 106

Agate, dyed

Appearances

Agate takes on color easily and often is turned blue, green, pink, and purple. While attractive, visually, I don't get any other vibes from dyed Agate. Compare a few dyed pieces with natural ones and you'll start to recognize the difference. Energetically, I've applied the word "appearances" to it, similar to Red Tiger Eye (another treated stone). It's an affected or cultivated appearance, like a carefully chosen wardrobe.

IMAGE 101 bright orange, reddish, **dyed Agate** disk page 108

Agate, Mystic

The Genius of Dreams

This material may actually be a Carnelian. Agates are also Quartz-based and are more known for the finely outlined patterns you see in this variety. The Mystic Agates take this patterning to another level, though, in terms of fantasy and complexity. So, I would place them above plain Pattern Agate in terms of being a powerful Vision stone. Hence my tag of it as "the genius of dreams."

IMAGE 102 **Mystic Agate** page 109

Amethyst, dark

Reveal My Higher Purpose
(Spiritual Mission)

In the Healing energy zone, we have the lighter Lavender Amethyst. This is different. It's dark and it's all about fulfilling some intrinsic and meaningful purpose with your life. While some dark clusters could do, I prefer single points with rich color to explore this theme.

IMAGE 103 twin pair of **Dark Amethyst** points page 110

Apatite, blue

The Stuff of Dreams and Visions
(Subconscious)

Not much I can add to the statements above. This one's like a direct junction box into not only our individual subconscious, but the collective sub-conscious (or collective mind). As Mystic Agate could be the detail of our dreams, Blue Apatite is the source and inspiration for them.

IMAGE 104 sphere of **Blue Apatite** page 111

Calcite, optical

A Second Glance

These are rhomboid shapes, cubes that lean over, and that do funny things to images when you hold one over them. Because of its messing with our vision, I put it in this section. And it's cool. But beyond that, it's more of a specimen or oddity than a metaphysically powerful tool (for me at least). A member of one of my med-

IMAGE 157   SOURCE

RECORD KEEPERS on a growth interference **NIRVANA QUARTZ** (India), more on page 61 + 178
Portals to Knowledge

itation groups gave me a good idea for it—since it jogs an image over—why not think of it as an alternate view or perspective. I like that, and it confirms for me that it belongs here in Vision rather than in Channel.

Charoite

From Siberia, this unique and occasionally chatoyant (plays with the light) stone is here in Vision because of that visual quality. But I have honestly not yet cracked the code or mystery of what more there is to know about Charoite except that it is purple, it's beautiful, and I can tell it's powerful. As soon as I do figure it out, you can be sure I'll be sharing what I learn with the world.

IMAGE 168 cylinder of **Charoite** page 177

Fluorite, indigo

Twilight without Judgement

Indigo Fluorite is akin to Blue Apatite, Iolite, and Shattuckite—they all tap into the subconscious in slightly different ways. I can't really say more than that, except that I'll draw for each as the mood strikes.

IMAGE 105 **Indigo Fluorite** chunk page 112

Fluorite, purple

Purple Fluorite ought by right to be a key Vision stone akin to Dark Amethyst, but Amethyst has primacy because its color is more pure and powerful (in my experience).

Iolite

May be grouped with the stones mentioned earlier, including Indigo Fluorite and possibly Tanzanite as well.

Jasper, Ocean

The Inventiveness of Nature

A very visual experience, comparable to Rhyolite and Pattern Agate. It's also called Orbicular Jasper because it is riddled with circular patterns. Another favorite among Jaspers, and powerful enough to have been given the defining phrase above, about representing the inventiveness of nature.

IMAGE 106 **Ocean Jasper** sphere page 113

ROOT   IMAGE 158

TRIGONIC FORMATIONS on a **RUBY CRYSTAL** (India), more on page 62 + 118

Divine Geometric Intervention

Labradorite

Letting the Subconscious Through
(Imagination)

For the price, Labradorite can't be beat for connecting us with our imagination and creativity. It comes primarily from Madagascar but was originally named after the first discoveries in Canada. Finland has its own version of this called Spectrolite, which I think of as more linear in its color scheme. Malagasy (from Madagascar) Labradorite can flash red, green, blue, purple, pink, yellow, and orange (basically the whole rainbow of colors). Most often the color spread is abstract and flowing, but sometimes it's linear and the stone seems to have colored grills or lines running through it. The background stone can be a greenish black or a grayish blue (in which case I call it Blue Labradorite). It's cut into every imaginable shape, looks great in jewelry, and I particularly like a polished piece that's backed by the rough chunk. Seeing the color flash through the smooth side is easy, but when it comes through the natural rough side, it's an unusual treat.

IMAGE 107 **Labradorite** palm piece page 114

Lodolite, Garden, or Gazer Quartz

These Quartzes have inclusions in them that look like little garden dioramas and generally show best if some part of the stone has been polished. So the polished part is forward, say at the top of a cabochon or palm piece, and the scenery that gives it interest consists of inclusions and irregularities in the back or base of the stone (which you can see inside, like you're looking into an aquarium). In the future I'll capture one of these on film.

Moonstone, white or rainbow

The good stuff goes pretty exclusively into jewelry, but it's nice and has a higher vibration than Labradorite. Labradorite is more all over the place—in a good way—but in order to focus on the moon energy or a tightened scope of the spectrum (i.e. shimmery white), there's nothing like Moonstone. I've mentioned other Moonstones (chocolate, silver and black for example) as being like lenses or filters into different aspects of our personal energy spectrum. In this case, the Rainbow Moonstone is like a window into the Vision energy zone, shedding light on it like the moon in the night sky.

IMAGE 159   SOURCE

CLEAVED OCTAHEDRON of
GREEN FLUORITE (South Africa),
more on page 62 + 174
The Balance of Heaven and Earth

Obsidian, Rainbow

Rainbow Obsidian is a particularly evocative variety. It's got layers that catch and throw back light, particularly in bright light, revealing patterns in polished pieces. One particular way of cutting it allows you to see hearts, which are quite unique and spectacular. When the colors shimmer or seem to add a three dimensional quality, I call these lucent. When the lines are visible even when the piece is not lit up, and there's no movement or flash in them, I call this the chromatic variety.

Natrolite

This stone (as I've seen it) seems to combine Rainbow Moonstone with the purest translucent lavender, such as you'd see in a gemmy Labradorite. I like it, but would need larger samples to understand it better.

Opal, Ethiopian or colored

From the Concrete to the Most Etheric
(Multiple Dimensions, Infinite Potentials)

Very powerful stuff. I've recently separated Australian from Ethiopian Opal, but mostly the distinction I'm making is between the lighter, creamier or whiter material and the more colorful material. Each source has both. When an Opal has lots of flash and color, I consider it tapping into both multiple dimensions and our infinite potential.

IMAGE 108 large **Ethiopian Opal** floater page 115

Rhyolite

Rhyolite offers a range of different pattern types. It can look more like a Sandstone and more like an Ocean Jasper. I don't particularly find it more useful than the other types, but it is a distinctive variety.

Seraphinite

Discovering the Unknown

Kind of like a green Charoite, a bit more chatoyant (plays with light when you turn it) and with more fantastic patterns. This is another stone from Russia that I have not spent nearly enough time with to speak more intelligently about. I like it a lot though. And I have gotten a strong hit about it facilitating journeying.

IMAGE 109 radial pattern **Seraphinite** display piece page 116

Shattuckite

Shield of the Subconscious

Shattuckite looks a lot like Chrysocolla, but it tends to be darker, a bit more on the indigo side of the spectrum. That brings it up from Voice to Vision and it's one of my favorites for tapping into the subconscious. I do call it the shield of the subconscious because I think of it as somewhat of a gatekeeper.

IMAGE 110 photo of Congolese **Shattuckite** page 117

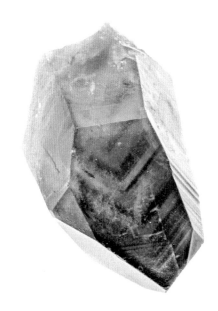

IMAGE 161	FOUNDATION

PHANTOM formations in **GREEN CITRINE** (Brazil), more on page 64 + 126

Integrating Past Life-Experience

Sodalite

Sodalite is a lesser version of Lapis and although I tend to ignore it, I have begun to think it as a Vision stone rather than a Voice stone (like Lapis). That means it joins some of the other stones in this zone like Shattuckite, Apatite, and Indigo Fluorite having to do with access to the subsconscious.

Tanzanite

I have never spent time with Tanzanite, the quality crystals are too astronomically expensive, but I sense that it's a Vision stone rather than a Source stone. It has too much notoriety not to be mentioned here.

Ulexite

Akin to a very high-quality Selenite, this material is also called TV stone because it projects images up from under it, to its top surface. This is rather surreal and convinced me to place it here as a Vision stone. It could also arguably be a Channel stone, but I haven't spent enough time with it to move it from here. I group it with Optical Calcite, they share a very similar visual dynamic.

9. SOURCE — SPIRIT

I like to think of Vision as the path, and Source as the destination. We use our imaginations to get to the places we want to go. Ultimately, if you're spiritually inclined, Source is somewhere very interesting and attractive to want to visit and spend time in.

Note also that Source and Foundation are very similar words. Our foundation is our source. When we reach the highest places, we can see how they connect and recycle through the lowest places.

Ajoite

This is a fabulously expensive clear Quartz (hops quickly into the thousands of dollars for small crystals) with bright blue flecks in it. I have no energetic read on it because I sometimes avoid cult stones that have a lot of hype around them (that I can't immediately relate to). If I did have to assess it vibrationally, just from looking at it, I would suggest that it combines the qualities of Clear Quartz with those of Turquoise, a kind of magnification and clarification of self-compassion. Those are pretty great qualities after all, but I can also access them using a more plentiful Clear Quartz and a nice piece of Turquoise.

Apophyllite, green

Much more rare than white Apophyllite, green Apophyllite combines Vision and Source elements, blending path and destination interestingly.

Area 51 Stone

Relics of Visitation

Fable has it that this pseudomorph (started as something and turned into something else) was picked up surreptitiously off the highway that goes by Roswell (New Mexico)—where the aliens were said to have been found—by a guy who threw a bunch of dirt into his trunk. When he sorted through it later, he found these six-sided nuggets of Dolomite. You know me, I'm not tempted to buy into the hype of this stone also known as Roswellite. But you have to feel these stones to believe them. They are truly otherworldly and reminiscent of a post-apocalyptic bloom or stone flower.

IMAGE 111 **Area 51** stone page 118

Astrophyllite

Shooting Stars Reflection

I really like this material because it has starburst metallic filaments throughout it and clearly looks mysterious, but I haven't worked with it explicitly and so I have nothing more to add (currently) about that. I certainly look forward to learning more, it's definitely intriguing. What I can say, is that it resembles shooting stars, hence my tag line for it above.

IMAGE 112 **Astrophyllite** obelisk page 119

Azurite

Let Me See Where I Cannot Go
(Other Worlds)

Azurite seems to be found in two forms: crystallized bundles, ideally in starburst floaters (from China and the U.S.); and a more massive, less crystallized, and tumbled form from Africa. It's very otherworldly and high in vibration.

IMAGE 113 **Azurite** starburst floater page 120

IMAGE 162   CHANNEL

GROWTH INTERFERENCE QUARTZ
(Russia), more on page 65 + 187

The Path Less Chosen

Beta Quartz

Although rare, the octahedral crystal form (pyramid-above-and-pyramid-below) is surpassed in rarity by this Quartz wonder. It has six sides on top matched symmetrically by six sides underneath. Because of my reverence for the octahedron as a religious symbol for the Crystal World, it stands to reason that I should automatically treasure Beta Quartz. I've seen wonderful but small pieces come out of Indonesia in large quantities (but of variable quality), more rare Prase (green) versions from Siberia, and I own a couple of bigger ones from China. I have Beta Quartz terminations in an Indian cluster, and recently bought a Herkimer Diamond that would be a perfect Beta Quartz if not for its flattened "belt" around the middle.

IMAGE 154 larger **Beta Quartz** from China page 161

Blue Crystallized Quartz

Frozen Flow

Different from the massive material listed in Voice, this is exceedingly rare and high vibration. Some of my Prase Quartz was sold to me as blue, but it's not this blue. For Quartz to crystallize in blue is more unusual than into pink, red, or green. It's kind of like Azurite, representing a separate, galactic residence or planet frozen in time.

IMAGE 153 starburst floater of **Blue Crystallized Quartz** page 160

Cassiterite

I have a couple of pieces of this material and have seen a few lesser specimens of it, but it's so powerful I had to include it here. It's heavy and has a ridge top to its termination like Topaz, but then the surface of the crystal is draped with downward arched record keepers. Quite special!

Cavansite

Akin to Azurite but usually tiny, these bright blue starburst crystal formations are fragile but exquisite. They are like precious, high vibration flower blossoms. I could use a big Cavansite floater, but we have to be satisfied with the fact that they're mostly small.

Celestial Quartz

Beam up to the Stratosphere

I've had trouble capturing images of these for publication, something about them seems to defy the focusing capabilities of even the best cameras. These are shards of Quartz that don't terminate traditionally, but they're terminated all around as floaters (no break points). Nobody else that I know of has identified these as a separate form or worthy of attention, but they are super high vibration and happen in Quartz, ultra-clear Quartz, and Smoky Quartz (that I've seen so far).

IMAGE 114 shard of **Celestial Quartz** page 121

ROOT   IMAGE 163

BORTRYOIDAL formation of HEMATITE (Morocco), more on page 66 + 113

My Cup Runneth Over

Chrysanthemum Stone

Starbeams from Home

I was originally turned on to these by the Moroccan version. A white spiky sun representation on a stark black background. I came to think they were drawn on and certainly enhanced. I was surprised to see a broken one that showed the white was actually a radiating crystal, so I'm not sure what to believe there anymore. They are cool looking, but simply not as authentic in feel as the Chinese Chrysanthemum Stones (pictured in this book) which are far more abstract in their starburst shapes and the black matrix stone does not seem like it's been painted. Finding well-formed, harmonious shapes can be tough, but it's worth it. I have a whole range of small Chrysanthemum Stone pendants that look like little white fireworks in the sky. In any case, I take these to represent our home in the stars (or at least our view of them).

IMAGE 115 **Chrysanthemum Stone** display piece page 122

Dream Quartz

(Spirit Mansions) *Other Dimensional Dwellings*

Epidote or Actinolite—not actual crystals, but some finer form of them—colors these Quartz formations from Madagascar. They are generally tabular and floaters, akin to Prase Quartz because they're both green and mysterious, but found on different continents.

IMAGE 116 **Dream Quartz** mansion page 123

Fluorite, aquamarine

(Watery Mediums) *Furthest Depths, Below and Beyond*

This is one of my favorite forms of Fluorite. Of course it is not actually an Aquamarine, it is simply the color aquamarine, featuring the

IMAGE 164   SELF

ETCHED AMETRINE standing twin
(Bolivia), more on page 67 + 122

Shaped by Time

blend or banding of blue and green for a stunning combination. I can't say enough—or as much here as I might want to—about how special this material is. What I will say is that it takes the subconscious of the mind and projects it downward, into the depths of the sea. It is a Source stone that is located below the surface of the waters. Physically, the material comes from Mexico uniquely, though there is also Aquamarine Fluorite, mostly in rainbow form—slabs and such—to be had from China.

IMAGE 117 pair of connected **Aquamarine Fluorite** hearts page 124

Fluorite, blue

(Higher Communication)
May I Be Higher Consciousness

I really like Blue Fluorite. It's got a very gentle vibe, not quite as intense for me as the green. Although you could choose it if you were more of a "blue person" than a "green person," I give it a slightly different energy signature than Green Fluorite (described below). If Aquamarine (the actual stone) is about higher mind communication, and Gem Silica is about intra-spirit communication, Blue Fluorite could be a go between, or third level or corner of this communication triangle. China has Blue Fluorite, but the one we've featured in this book is one of the rare and wonderful Illinois Fluorites. There is a third type that is worth mentioning, New Mexico Blue Fluorite, which I would suggest opens up a new way of understanding Blue Fluorite as a Source stone for healing (or a Healing stone for Source).

IMAGE 118 octahedral collector specimen of
Illinois blue Fluorite page 125

FOUNDATION   IMAGE 165

MERKABA form in AURALITE (India),
more on page 68 + 108
Essential Sacred Geometry

Fluorite, green

Connecting with My Guides
(Spirit Community)

Closer to this earthly plane than Moldavite, Green Fluorite is a giant for me. It holds the very important role of representing the place, space, or medium where we can encounter and be with our spirit community, whatever that means for us. If you don't consider yourself connected to a higher spirit community, this could be your gateway. If you are, this is the happy place or playground to commune with and relate to your guides.

Most Green Fluorite (particularly polished material) comes from China, with some very rich (and octahedral) material coming from South Africa. Historically, the Wise Mine in New Hampshire (U.S.), produced a huge amount of Green Fluorite, which is my favorite, energetically.

When I speak of Green Fluorite, I mean Fluorite that is mostly green, not Rainbow Fluorite. Rainbow Fluorite is a mix, often featuring purple, and is interesting mostly because of its combination of colors and energies.

IMAGE 119 Chinese **Green Fluorite** cluster coated with **record keepers** page 126 and **octahedron** page 167

Heulandite

The DNA of Crystals

Heulandite is a pretty hard to find crystal from India and rarely forms as exquisitely as the one we've chosen to picture here in this book. Because it's green, it has the elder/ancestor appeal of Prase Quartz but is unusual because its crystals can be twisted or rounded, which gives it an added element of mystery. Have a look at the photo to see why I called it the DNA of crystals.

IMAGE 120 double helix **Heulandite** crystal page 127

Lemurian Quartz

Among the Spiritual Leaders
(The Mantle of Governance)

At first, I was put off by the notion of it being a "seed crystal" dropped strategically around the globe by either aliens or Lemurians (a lost civilization here on earth, of which there is no record). But after customers' interest got me buying them, I was sold. I now have the largest Lemurian selection I've ever seen. My blog on the topic is very popular online and I've realized that this is the only clear Quartz that lives in the Source energy zone.

IMAGE 166   HEALING

BOWL of BLUE CACITE (Madagascar), more on page 68 + 142

Scoop of Peace

What makes Lemurians different is twofold. First is their distinctive termination style. The points tend to be made up of three touching faces and the other three of these—what I call facet faces on the point—are set back. Some people think it's the ridges along their sides that makes them Lemurians—which they often have, but so does Arkansas Quartz (which produces few Lemurians). Lemurians often have an extra face or facet beyond the usual six at the top. They sometimes have dolphining, where a side takes a sudden curvy dip, but most often you can tell a Lemurian if the actual siding varies dramatically in shape from side to side. Looking through a semi-rectangular side, you might see a much tighter triangle in back, which is the opposite side. And often Lemurians will alternate clear and frosty siding. If a Quartz has most or all of these six qualifying factors, it's most likely a Lemurian.

Lemurians mostly come from Brazil, but very impressively (in terms of shape and clarity) originate from Colombia as well. Morocco has mostly red iron coated ones and you'll occasionally find Indian, American, and Malagasy Lemurians.

The second distinctive quality I wanted to share about Lemurians is that they are Entity Stones, not necessarily housing an individual, but almost like the role of an individual. Just as royalty takes on titles, or someone is a congressperson for a time, the Lemurians are holding those positions. By working with them, we are able to put that status or mantle on to work for, or rather with us.

IMAGES 121 + 171 **three-sided Lemurian Quartz** (Muzo habit or shape) pages 128 + 180

Image 141 **Lemurian Quartz** generator page 153

HEART   IMAGE 167

PALM PIECE of ROSE QUARTZ (Madagascar), more on page 70 + 136

One-to-One Stone Communicator

Libyan Gold Tektite

Also known as Libyan Desert Glass (giving it the initials LGT or LDG), these Tektites blend space elements with sand from the desert to produce a pale to rich yellow meteoric glass. These have enjoyed a lot of attention recently—and I like them, to be sure—but they are not equal for me to the other, darker Tektites from elsewhere in the world. Yes, they're different and have equal status as all stones do. I'm just saying, in my system, they don't yet have an important place.

Merlinite

Develop your Wizardry

Also known in the geology books as Gabbro, Merlinite has the powerful distinction of including black, white, and purple. For me that means it's able to navigate the dark and the light with wisdom. The wisdom I speak of is like that of a wizard or witch, capable of conjuring and protecting themselves. I recommend folks facing black magic to school themselves with some defense against the dark arts, a la Harry Potter. And Merlinite is the stone to represent that process of learning and implementing such skills.

IMAGE 122 **Merlinite** chunk page 129

Moldavite

Messages from On High
(Alien Energy)

Where to begin on this!? I have blogs, podcasts, and videos devoted to Moldavite. You'll see from my breakthrough story, it's how I got turned on to crystals in the first place. Right now, I'm really getting into larger specimens and am filling out my selection to rival what I have for Jade and Sugilite, in terms of price ranges and world class specimens. Recent pieces I've bought have nicknames like Life, The Forest, Cosmic Lake, and even the Galactic Trilobite. These are not for beginners, and yet—as in my case—any Moldavite might become the perfect "gateway drug." The key, and what it's all about, is the message. Moldavites are messengers, so you have to figure out what message each one you have is carrying for you, and to apply the lessons or dictates of that message in your life.

Moldavites are reproduced and you can buy fakes of it. Certifications don't necessarily prove that they're real. You can trust your source or get it appraised by a qualified gemologist. Once you start seeing a lot of them, though, you can tell without anyone else confirming it for you whether they're real or not.

Two big things in the Moldavite world are gram weight and locality. Each increment over 20 grams, up to a maximum of just over 100 grams tops, is that much more rare than the smaller size dimension.

IMAGE 168   VISION

CYLINDER of CHAROITE
(Russia), more on page 71 + 166
Spiritual Column

So, people note and publicize gram weight as a matter of course for context on size. Next in importance, is the locality where the specimen was found, which can make a huge difference in how they look. Different soils and conditions have altered their faces tremendously over literally millions of years. Some are almost smooth but have super complex and tiny craters and fissures in them, like a Zatacka Moldavite. Or as in the case of the Besednices, they can have super raised ridges like a hedgehog, all over them.

IMAGE 123 spiky (14 gram) **Besednice Moldavite** drop or leaf page 130

Image 177 **Chlum Moldavite** (40+ grams) pendant necklace page 198

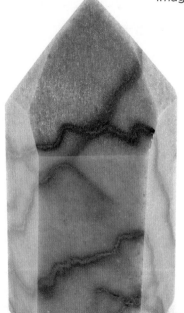

VOICE   IMAGE 169

GENERATOR of BLUE QUARTZ
(Brazil), more on page 73 + 158

Communication Potential

Nebulite

Galactic Federations

I've renamed this fascinating Chrome Chalcedony from Turkey, Nebulite, because it looks like some sort of galactic formation. I've used it to great effect to get people quite high, energetically, in meditation.

IMAGE 124 **Nebulite Chrome Chalcedony** page 131

Nirvana Quartz

Greater Human Earth Essence
(The Oversoul Spirits)

A giant that didn't make it into the card deck, but surely will for the next, is the Growth Interference Nirvana Quartz. They are six-sided but rarely have any proper points and they're heavily etched. Also called Glacier Quartz, they are even deeper than Elestial Quartz in terms of wisdom (partly due to their infinite nooks and crannies that seem to hold knowledge). Found first in the Himalayas, where they were also called (if the color merited it) Pink Kulu Quartz, I have also acquired versions of it from Brazil and Zimbabwe.

IMAGE 125 **African Nirvana Quartz** page 132

IMAGE 157 **Himalayan Nirvana Quartz** page 165

Peridot

Its crystals can be small and it shows up in jewelry a lot. I would love a big piece to fully assess its properties. Given all the other green stones I have to work with, I have neglected it. It's also called Olivine, when it's not gem quality. Olivine appears in Pallasite meteorites. I do have some specimens that are basically like druzy Quartz (small glittery terminations covering a surface) but green.

Phenacite

I've steered clear of this stone for decades, turned off by the cost and the hype around it. I finally bought some Brazilian and Burmese crystals that were decently formed, and I could be convinced. They're like (especially the Brazilian one) a cross between Topaz and Quartz, very high vibration. The Burmese are these little rook-like crystals with undulating terminations that look like they've been filed, and they're much wispier, vibrationally.

Prase Quartz

Colored and impacted (in its crystal formation) by Hedenburgite and/or Actinolite, this is one of the most powerful of the Quartzes. The photo I have of this material perfectly demonstrates what a cathedral Quartz should look like (with precise triangular terminations all up its side). Originally, this type was called Prasem Quartz and showed up in Greece on the island of Serifos. Fortunately for those of us who love it, recent decades have uncovered sources in Inner Mongolia that have yielded extraordinary specimens (though not so much over the past few years). What I love about Prase Quartz is the extraordinarily complex surfacing, which makes it akin to Nirvana Quartz, etched Quartz, and Elestial Quartz. I'm also impressed that this is alone among green Quartzes in terms of its perfect crystallization (and uniform coloration). Aventurine, for example, is thoroughly green but never crystallizes.

IMAGE 160 cathedral **Prase Quartz** page 168

Prasiolite

Occurring naturally and artificially (through treatments, for inclusion in jewelry) this Green Amethyst has a very high vibration. It's a translucent green Quartz, unlike Dream and Prase Quartzes, but certainly is an ascension stone I've used for Source meditations and activities. Such activities or agendas include connecting with spirits, traveling in higher realms, and bringing down messages from on high (like Moldavite). Prasiolite is like a Quartz version of Green Apophyllite.

IMAGE 170   SELF

OBELISK of AMETRINE (Bolivia), more on page 74 + 122

Self in Spirit

Pyrite Concretion

Alignment of Beings in the Earth

The way I describe these is that minerals pooled underground and the crystallizing Pyrite rings were "sweated out" in concentric bead rings around the stone. I've only sold these to shamans and serious energy workers who immediately recognize this variety's capabilities in terms of grounding us into the earth and yet also sourcing energy from our relationship with it.

IMAGE 126 unusual infinity-form **Pyrite Concretion** page 133

Selenite, diamond and flying

Space Stations Here and There

In the Channel energy zone, we have the standard Moroccan Selenite. In the Healing energy zone, we have some Naica healing Selenite. Here, we feature two sort of stand-alone specimens that have attained Source status because they place us somewhere else, somewhere very highly elevated and caught up in much larger galactic dynamics. You can tell this simply by looking at these pieces and imagining working with them in the center of a stone layout or constellation.

IMAGE 127 **Diamond Selenite** from Nevada page 134

IMAGE 128 **Flying Selenite**, most likely from Mexico page 135

Spinel, octahedral

This is one of those crystals that form into my revered octahedral shape. Colors can range from pink and red to black, blue, and brown. While the shape lands it in Source, the colors and dense feel of the stone can resemble Ruby and Sapphire and be grounding in a spiritual way, which is a kind of cool duality. Sometimes Spinel appears in other stones and looks a bit like embedded Ruby crystals.

CHANNEL   IMAGE 171

WAND of 3-sided Lemurian Quartz (Brazil), more on page 57 + 74

Streamlining Intention

Spirit Quartz

Cosmic Wand

Often confused with Cactus Quartz, or considered the same thing, I define Spirit Quartz as Quartz (also from South Africa) that has fine tiny points or druzy Quartz all over it. This makes it look a bit like sandpaper but does not take away from the overall shape of the primary point. I think the name is good, it certainly does have a higher vibration, which puts it here in the Source energy zone. But beyond that, it's not one of my go-to crystals.

IMAGE 129 **Spirit Quartz** transmitter page 136

Spodumene, Triphane and Hiddenite

There are two varieties of Spodumene that I will address here. I have a superior Triphane nicknamed Angel Finger. It's a double terminated and three-sided single crystal that only a few people ever get to see. It is the light green version of the generally yellow variety of Spodumene, made famous by the pink variety Kunzite. Hiddenite is the explicitly green variety of Spodumene and can also be quite special, but I've only seen rough, beat up specimens of it. My Triphane is green, so I'm talking about it here because I imagine it is more like what an ideal Hiddenite would look like. I rarely have a need for the Angel Finger, but there's nothing like it for being touched by spirit in a meditation or healing.

Tourmaline, blue

Also known as Indicolite, this may be the rarest form of Tourmaline, which could explain why I don't have any. Some have passed through my hands, but none big enough (though I've seen some big ones) that I could get a real read for what it had to say energetically.

Tourmaline, green

I have long been a non-fan of Green Tourmaline. I think it's overrated and overpriced, so I never bought a piece capable of sharing its charge with me. I've also shied away from it because I have so many other great green stones to play with. That being said, one day—as finances allow—I will buy some proper Tourmalines. In the meantime, I mostly traffic in smaller and black specimens, which people appreciate.

IMAGE 130 **Green Tourmaline** page 137

Zincite

Vision in Source

An industrial Zinc byproduct found in the inefficient exhaust smokestacks of Poland in the middle of the last century. I couldn't make that up if I tried! It's pretty obscure in its sourcing, but wonderful stuff nonetheless. It doesn't have that totally artificial vibe like the Aura Quartzes, maybe because it was not exclusively manufactured for sale but happened naturally as a result of some other process going on independently. It's very grounding and yet somehow creative. I think of it as a Vision stone for the Source Zone, but I'm not sure that designation will stick. My favorite specimens have been a rich orange, like the one pictured in this book, or an almost metallic glittery silver color.

IMAGE 131 standing **Orange Zincite** page 138

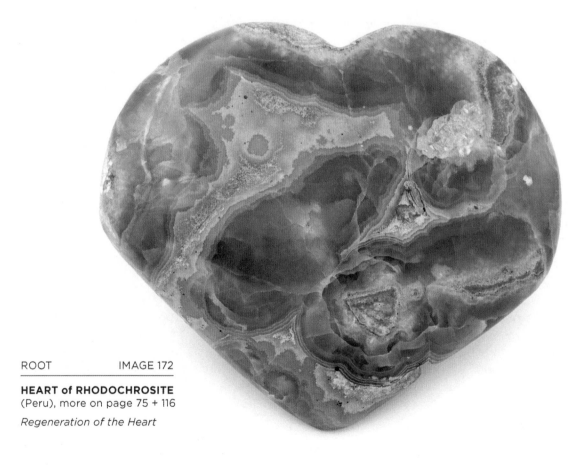

ROOT   IMAGE 172

HEART of RHODOCHROSITE
(Peru), more on page 75 + 116
Regeneration of the Heart

10. CHANNEL FLOW

Apophyllite, clear

May I Be There, Now
(Astral Plane)

Softer and more brittle than Quartz, Apophyllite proves that you don't have to have the strongest wings to fly high. I believe it's perfect for psychics to get into that higher place where spirits dwell. I've also called it The Elevator because it can take you up 50 flights before you know it.

Apophyllite comes from India and, while its clusters are great, I prefer single points knocked off the clusters. They make great third eye stones. And they stand like little natural pyramid generators without any cutting or polishing needed.

IMAGE 132 **Apophyllite** generator point page 139

Aura Quartz

Being Beyond Incarnation
(The Disembodied Self or Supranatural Ego)

There are many types of Aura Quartz. The original one was Aqua Aura, supposedly made with Gold dust. They're all plated in a vacuum chamber at high heat. Some cheap versions are probably coated in some other way. I believe Titanium and Cobalt are other precious metals they fuse to the surface of clear Quartz, turning it into other Aura varieties. Now they've started doing this with other stones like Amethyst, Hematite, and Danburite.

I've found that this treatment masks or eliminates the stone's original energy signature. It lends a ghostly overlay. For being named Aura, it's more like an anti-aura. It's quite ungrounding, and is in the Channel zone because disembodiment is ultimately a modulation of energy. I never have use for that, but I can see how someone might. Also, it's pretty, and that's generally the number one determinant of whether someone will buy something. That's why they keep making it.

IMAGE 133 **Aura Quartz** page 140

Black Tourmaline

My Borders Are Clear
(Bumper, Limits)

The most basic protection stone, Black Tourmaline comes from Brazil, China, Madagascar, and parts of Africa. It can be poorly formed and flaky or very tight and with shiny clear terminations. It's also called Schorl. It's a key and basic protection stone used to set boundaries. It's one of those, like Selenite, that makes sense to place in the four corners of your home.

IMAGE 151 standing double terminated **Black Tourmaline** battery crystal page 158

Black Tourmalinated Quartz

Compassionate Limits
(Omnidirectional Boundaries)

Amazingly, Black Tourmaline is able to run its way through Quartz in seemingly random directions—something it cannot do outside of Quartz. The result, particularly when consistently spread out through the Quartz, can be stunning. This is also effective as a whole different way of experiencing Black Tourmaline, which is usually a one-liner, whether in single crystals or in a chunk. The introduction of a multi-axis presentation of Black Tourmaline means that it's possible to interpret it as providing those types of boundaries in all directions but with compassion, given the fact that the Quartz it forms in is usually milky. Milky Quartz is a Heart stone associated with compassion.

IMAGE 134 **Black Tourmalinated** sphere page 141

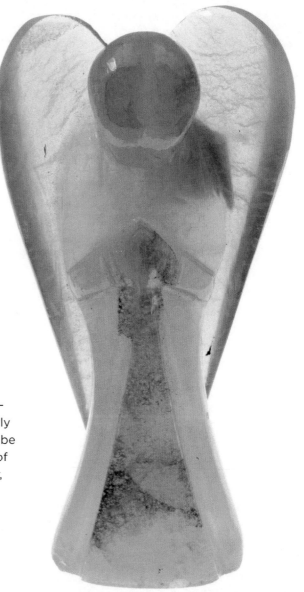

SELF + CHANNEL   IMAGE 173

ANGEL of **YELLOW FLUORITE** (Argentina), more on page 76 + 124

Healing Light to the Self

Blue Tara Quartz

Channel Vision

I used to call this Wispy Blue Quartz because the Riebeckite (apparently) that runs through it is non-linear. Unlike Tourmaline and Rutile, it does not glow in straight lines, but instead looks like light blue-gray clouds wafting through the Quartz. Although I don't have a particular use for this material, I stockpile it because it's so rare, and I recognize that it adds an aspect of vision to the Source energy zone.

IMAGE 135 **Blue Tara Quartz** generator page 142

Cerussite

This is the only stone I actually find un-lifeful. It's essentially a translucent yellowish lead crystal. Hurts me when I hold it, literally, my nerve endings are unhappy. I think it could be useful, like chemotherapy, to fight and undermine unwanted intruders in the system. But like Irradiated Quartz, you'd have to be careful, and mindful with it. Recently, I used it in a meditation, and learned that a lesson it could teach is how to be with the energy of serious illness (actually sit with and accept the disease on some level). This application could really make it useful.

Diamantina laser Quartz

This is the legendary, natural laser wand from Diamantina Brazil. The points are quite distinctive. They are wider at the base and taper all the way up to the top, like two chopsticks apart at the bottom and connecting at the skinny end. At that top, there's a tiny point that completes the crystal. As a perfect laser, the Diamantina is particularly effective at channeling energy and intention.

These have also been called Singing Quartz, although any slim Quartzes that produce a high-pitched sound when tapped together could also be called Singing Quartz. In Moldavite, such pieces are called Angel Chime, because of the sounds they make even just moving them through your hands.

IMAGE 150 **Diamantina laser Quartz** point page 157

Entity Stones

Personality, Embodiment
(Possession)

These stones—which could be made of any type of material (ocean stones or Quartz, for example)—look like little beings. They might feature heads, mouths, eyes, or unusual body shapes. They are not meant to be exact reproductions of any type of person or animal. They have become, however, interim or permanent homes for unusual and possibly unsettled spirits. I've mentioned them in association with death, as a way station where a soul can reside, but navigating such manipulations of spirit can be treacherous.

IMAGE 136 **Entity Stone** page 143

Faden Quartz

Surviving the Interstitial Spaces

Faden in German refers to thread, or the milky center line that often runs through these tabular Quartz clusters that are attached to one another by the sides—sometimes standing spectacularly, but often jumbled together. I think of them as representing the tangents of our projects and undertakings, stitched together and growing in complicated ways through complex circumstances.

IMG. 152 **Faden Quartz** display crystals page 159

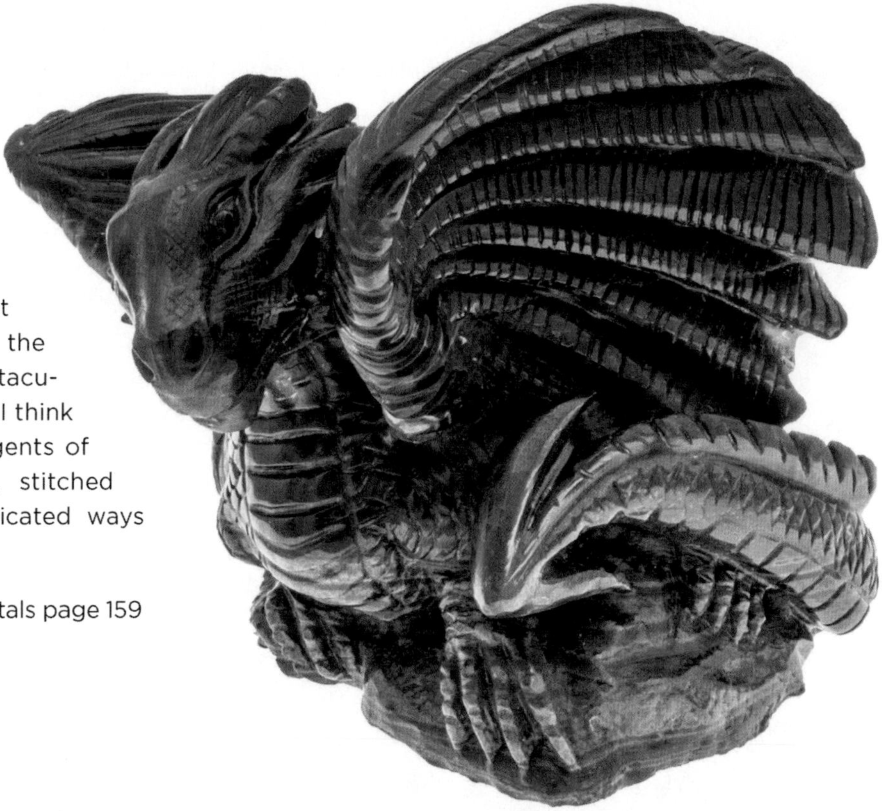

Fairy Stones

Develop, Adapt, Change
(Transformation)

Formed apparently from the excretion of an obscure lake bottom bacteria 10,000 years ago, these are found in Quebec (Canada) and Vermont. Also called Glacial Concretions, they may be a consequence of the ending Ice Age. France has a similar looking material called a Gogotte, but it grows larger and they claim it's formed some other way (which I doubt, 'cause they look the same). I consider many of these to be Entity Stones, but what I like most is that they sometimes seem to resemble dividing cells, hence the energetic description and affirmation I've given them above.

IMAGE 137 **Fairy Stone** concretion page 144

CHANNEL + SOURCE   IMAGE 174

ANIMAL CARVING SUGILITE DRAGON
(South African stone, carved in Thailand), more on page 77 + 162

The Beast, Captured only in Form

Growth Interference Quartz

The Path Less Chosen

There are places in the world where Quartz manages not to crystallize in even the myriad ways we have showcased in this book. They don't come to a natural point. I just discovered a type from Brazil that grows randomly and amorphously out of the side of larger crystals. One could also call it atypical growth and the Nirvana Quartzes are a good example of one direction this form can take.

IMAGE 162 **Growth Interference Quartz** from Russia page 171

Irradiated Quartz

Not Just on the Defense
(The Warrior)

I call these the attack dog of the Crystal World. They were clear Quartzes that were put through radiation chambers to artificially turn them black. The result is a very dangerous being that I've used for decades to protect my space. You just don't want to point it at yourself or any loved ones. They have one purpose, so you want to save them for that.

There is a huge amount of Irradiated Quartz out there being sold as natural Smoky Quartz. You can tell the difference because the bottoms or bases of the clusters are often not as dark. The irradiation process seems to work best on higher quality or, ironically, clear Quartz. Smoky Quartz is rarely found in clusters anyhow, so you can be pretty confident that a super dark Smoky Quartz cluster is actually irradiated.

IMAGE 138 large **Irradiated Quartz** I've had for 30 years page 145

Kyanite, black

Sweep out the Bad
(The Psychic Fan)

When I find a blockage, I use this to extract what's not moving and move it along. Always in a fan shape, this material looks a lot like a broom. Large well-formed pieces are hard to find, but worth it, 'cause I think they're more effective.

IMAGE 139 larger **Black Kyanite** fan page 146

Larvikite

Take Back Your Ill-intent
(Defensive Reflector)

This stone is like a mirror, putting back onto malefactors their own bad wishes. The affirmation above also cautions us to be mindful of where we put our own anger, lest it backfire on us. Larvikite looks more like a monochromatic gray Merlinite with more reflectivity. I think it's actually used for countertops and have learned that it was named after a place in Norway called Larvik Fjord.

IMAGE 140 **Larvikite** massage wand page 147

HEART + CHANNEL   IMAGE 175

DEITY, NEPHRITE JADE BUDDHA
(Australia), more on page 77 + 132
Higher Guides, Personified

Moonstone, multitone

Full Chakra Filter

I love the untraditional Moonstones. Peach is mentioned in the Belly energy zone, Rainbow in Vision, but there are others: green, chocolate, silver, and black come to mind. Several are featured in the actual stone we've pictured in this book, which speaks to the possibility that Moonstone reflects and acts as a filter or tonic for all the Energy Zones. Rather than healing them each per se, it allows us to peer into each and shed light on it, much as the moonlight sheds light onto the night-filled earth.

IMAGE 141 multi-tone **Moonstone** page 148

Morion Smoky Quartz

(The Watcher)
Guardian on All Sides

Naturally irradiated Smoky—which all Smokies are already—occasionally go overboard and turn totally black. We have found some very nice Morions from New Hampshire, less wonderful but more plentiful ones from Brazil, and some exquisite ones from China. When they get to be a super almost matte finish, they double also as healing stones. They've fully overcome the onslaught of radioactivity. It's like they've come out the other side and can now help us in need, having learned—as we should—how to transmute toxicity.

IMAGE 142 New Hampshire **Morion Smoky Quartz** page 149

Nuumite

Turn Back the Unseen Attacker
(Cosmic Deflector)

For the attacker that you don't know is even there—behind your back, or a hater from near or far—I present you with Nuumite. Apparently, it comes in two forms. The one I am talking about is more common and has little reflective flecks in it. It's more of a long range protector.

IMAGE 143 glittery **Nuumite** wafer page 150

Obsidian, black

The Black before Creation
(Open Space, Possibility)

Many people confuse Black Obsidian for a protection stone. That's missing the point of what it's all about, which is something completely different. Black Obsidian is an open door. If that's how you want to protect yourself, have at it. Instead, I recommend Black Obsidian for new beginnings, starting fresh, and trying to clear out the old while bringing in the new.

IMAGE 144 large chunk of **Black Obsidian** page 151

Obsidian, silver and golden sheen

Something from Nothing
(Light in the Darkness)

Imagine the light from a distant star, taking millennia to even get close enough to become visible, where there was nothing before. Technically, this is a Voice dynamic I've just named. I'm talking about the creation of something, anything, even just light, from a place of void. It's not necessarily a planned thing, premeditated, or wished into existence. It's more primeval than that. It just happens. I would call this the creative element of the void, maybe an echo of the Big Bang.

IMAGE 145 **Golden Sheen Obsidian** sphere page 152

Orpiment

Look but Don't Touch
(Live Magma)

Also known as Getchelite or Arsenic Sulfide, this is poisonous if ingested. Orpiment is part of a small class of stones and elements we come across in the Crystal World whose dynamic is not life-full. It could, for this reason, be called temptation, because of the dangerous consequences of messing with it. I keep it around because some people have asked for it and bought it. It has metaphysical qualities I'm unaware of, beyond what I've said here. It's very bright and looks like molten lava, with a full color spread of oranges and reds.

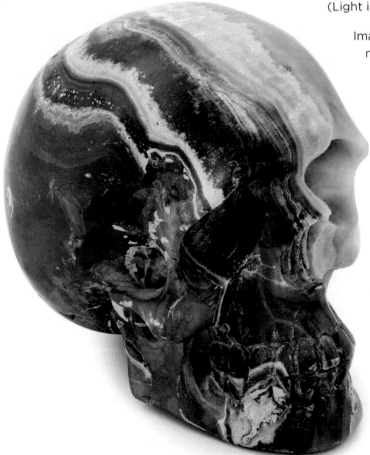

VISION   IMAGE 176

SKULL of **Bumblebee Jasper**
(Indonesia), more on page 78 + 123
Eternal Shell of the Soul

Quartz, clear

Direction with a Personal Twist
(Clarity, Focus)

Yes, Clear Quartz is here to help us to focus with clarity, but even polished pieces often have personality, unique inclusions inside, and points have distinctive exteriors to their terminations. That's why I mention the personal twist—it's particular to the crystal itself. Also, our relationship with it has the unique opportunity of having its own identity and trajectory. I like an ultra-clear tumbler or palm piece, it captures this essence well. Otherwise, most natural Quartzes come in handy as wands, generators, transmitters, etc.

IMAGE 146 standing, natural clear **Lemurian Quartz** generator page 153

Selenite, Moroccan

Clear Passage between Here and There
(An Open Conduit)

Many people swear by this generic type of Selenite. Every piece looks pretty much like every other piece. They must come out of big deposits to be chopped into bigger logs and then smaller-and-smaller logs and rods. Cut and tumbled happens a lot too. It does not terminate—or actually crystallize into points— from this source. But this Selenite is useful, especially for the price. It's relatively cheap.

I like a wide log or smaller, flat-surfaced piece to use as a balancing platform to align and stabilize pieces of jewelry or small tumblers. Works well to place crystals you've worked with too, to restore them to their original "settings." I don't tend to use it myself, though it's definitely neutral, incorruptible, and pure. I also like it as a way to create sacred space, if you arrange it to enclose and somewhere you're doing healing work. The energy moves along in a linear fashion, like fiber optics. That makes it a natural transmitter, so using it for protection doesn't make sense. It's also (just like with Black Obsidian) just like an open door. It doesn't hold energy, it merely allows energy to pass through it.

Shungite

Keeping Out the Bad
(The Filtering Stone)

I neglected to include this giant in my card decks thus far, but I won't make that mistake again. I like Shungite a lot. It's 98% Carbon and contains fullerenes (which I can't see and don't care about). I've always considered it to be petrified petroleum (which is not very romantic). Regardless of its formation—it's origin is primarily Russian—and while it has plenty of adoring literature and somewhat of a cult status, I think of it simply as an EMF protector and good to keep around for siphoning off unwanted energies.

IMAGE 147 **Shungite** sphere with **Pyrite** running through it page 154

Tektite, black

Own your Aura

Tektites (including Moldavite) are molten glass created from meteoric impacts and occur black throughout the world (except in Europe, interestingly, where Moldavite is green). My work with black Tektites (primarily from Asia) has shown me that it resonates with our aura-space. If you believe in and experience your aura, it runs from the surface of your skin (where your physical body leaves off) and extends out more (in feet) or less (in inches). That energy sheath is like the atmosphere is to the planet. And Tektites enable us to tune into and dwell in the enhanced presence and experience of our own aura.

IMAGE 148 **Black Tektite** page 155

Ventifact

Clearing the Pathway
(the Black Torch)

I bought a bunch of these in two shipments many years ago. They were in three sizes: small, medium, and huge. They are Basalt shards, mostly three-sided, that have been shaped and smoothed by thousands of years of wind and sand on the steppes of Argentina (towards the South Pole). "Venti" means wind and "fact" means made. If you tap them together, you get a high-pitched metallic clang, reminiscent of the Singing Quartz and Angel Chime Moldavite. I've worked a great deal with this stone and find it particularly useful for folks who are nervous about moving forward. It lights the way and knows the route better than you do. Also, it feels like it won't lead you wrong, like over a cliff.

IMAGE 149 large **Ventifact** shard page 156

Two-Category Master List

I thought it was very important to separate stones by energy zone in the previous list, so you could see each and read my various thoughts on the ones I think matter most. But because of all that detail, the listings spread out over many pages. Although each zone has their stones alphabetized, what follows ought to be an easy, quick reference guide to find what you're looking for more easily. Color-coding will make it easy to tell each stone's energy zone.

Rather than having one master list that would go on and on, I've split what would have been the exhaustive list roughly in half, grouping all the stones as either Quartz or non-Quartz. Quartz is very prolific on the planet and a lot of stones are Quartz that you wouldn't know without seeing them in this type of listing. So I believe that separating them in this way helps you to categorize them more easily.

QUARTZ

- Agate, Blue Lace (Healing)
- Agate, dyed (Vision)
- Agate, Mystic (Vision)
- Agate, patterned (Vision)
- Ajoite (Source)
- Amazez (Foundation)
- Amethyst, chevron (Healing)
- Amethyst, dark (Vision)
- Amethyst flower (Healing)
- Amethyst, light or lavender (Healing)
- Amethyst, pink (Healing)
- Ametrine (Self)
- Angel Phantom Quartz (Healing)
- Auralite (Foundation)
- Aura Quartz (Channel)
- Aventurine (Self)

- Beta Quartz (Source)
- Blue crystallized Quartz (Source)
- Blue Quartz (Voice)
- Blue Tara Quartz (Channel)
- Cactus Quartz (Healing)
- Candle Quartz (Healing)
- Carnelian, Mystic (Healing)
- Carnelian, red/orange (Belly)
- Carnelian, snowy (Healing)
- Celestial Quartz (Source)
- Chalcedony, indigo (Healing)
- Chalcedony, lavender (Healing)
- Chalcedony, pink (Healing)
- Citrine, natural (Self)
- "Citrine" faux: baked Amethyst (Belly)
- Diamantina laser Quartz (Channel)

- Dragon Quartz **(Root)**
- Dream Quartz (Source)
- Edenite, green 'rutile' Quartz **(Root)**
- Elestial Quartz **(Foundation)**
- Faden Quartz (Channel)
- Fenster Quartz (Healing)
- Gem Silica **(Voice)**
- Girasol or Foggy Quartz **(Voice)**
- Growth Interference Quartz (Channel)
- Herkimer Diamond (Healing)
- Irradiated Quartz (Channel)
- Laser Quartz (Channel)
- Lemurian Quartz (Source)
- Lithium Quartz (Healing)
- Lodolite, garden or gazer Quartz **(Vision)**
- Mango Quartz **(Belly)**
- Manifestation Quartz (Self)
- Milky Quartz **(Heart)**
- Moon Quartz (Healing)
- Morion Smoky Quartz (Channel)
- Nirvana Quartz (Source)
- Petrified Wood, black **(Foundation)**

- Petrified Wood, darker (Self)
- Petrified Wood, lighter (Self)
- Petrified Wood, red **(Root)**
- Phantom Quartz (Self)
- Prase Quartz (Source)
- Prasiolite aka Green Amethyst (Source)
- Quartz, clear (Channel)
- Red Cap Amethyst aka Super Seven, type 2 **(Root)**
- Red laser Quartz **(Root)**
- Relationship Stones (Heart), often but not always Quartz
- Rose Quartz **(Heart)**
- Rutilated Quartz, golden (Self)
- Skeletal or Fenster Quartz (Healing)
- Smoky Quartz **(Heart)**
- Spirit Quartz (Source)
- Super Seven (Self)
- Tangerine Quartz **(Belly)**
- Tanzurine Quartz **(Heart)**
- Thunder Bay Amethyst **(Root)**
- Vera Cruz Amethyst (Healing)
- Water Quartz (Healing)

NON-QUARTZ

- Amazonite **(Healing)**
- Amber **(Healing)**
- Ammonite **(Foundation)**
- Angelite aka blue Anhydrite **(Healing)**
- Apache Gold (Self)
- Apatite, blue **(Vision)**
- Apophyllite, green (Source)
- Apophyllite, white (Channel)
- Aquamarine **(Voice)**
- Aragonite, crystallized (Self)
- Aragonite, non-crystallized **(Healing)**
- Area 51 Stone (Source)
- Astrophyllite (Source)
- Azurite (Source)
- Barite, blue and brown **(Voice)**
- Bedrock **(Foundation)**
- Black Tourmalinated Quartz (Channel)
- Bloodstone **(Heart)**
- Bowenite **(Heart)**
- Calcite, blue **(Healing)**
- Calcite, Cobalto (Self)
- Calcite, honey or brown **(Belly)**
- Calcite, Mangano **(Healing)**
- Calcite, milky **(Healing)**
- Calcite, optical **(Vision)**
- Calcite, orange **(Belly)**
- Cassiterite (Source)
- Cavansite (Source)

- Celestite, blue **(Healing)**
- Celestite, white or ice (Source)
- Cerussite (Channel)
- Charoite **(Vision)**
- Chert, green **(Heart)**
- Chrome Chalcedony, Nebulite (Source)
- Chrysocolla **(Voice)**
- Chrysoprase **(Healing)**
- Cintamani Stone (Healing)
- Coquina, Hieroglyphic Jasper **(Foundation)**
- Danburite (Healing)
- Diamond (Source)
- Dianite **(Voice)**
- Dinosaur Bone **(Foundation)**
- Emerald **(Heart)**
- Entity Stones (Channel)
- Fairy Stones (Channel)
- Fluorite, amber (Self)
- Fluorite, aquamarine (Source)
- Fluorite, blue (Source)
- Fluorite, clear (Channel)
- Fluorite, green (Source)
- Fluorite, indigo **(Vision)**
- Fluorite, lavender (Healing)
- Fluorite, pink **(Healing)**
- Fluorite, purple **(Vision)**
- Fluorite, yellow (Self)
- Fossils **(Foundation)**

- Galena **(Root)**
- Garnet **(Root)**
- Gem Silica **(Voice)**
- Hanksite **(Voice)**
- Halite (Healing)
- Healers Gold (Self)
- Heliodor (Self)
- Hematite **(Root)**
- Hemimorphite (Healing)
- Heulandite (Source)
- Hiddenite aka green Spodumene (Source)
- Hypersthene (Self)
- Iolite **(Vision)**
- Jade, blue Jadeite **(Voice)**
- Jade, green Nephrite **(Heart)**
- Jade, white Siberian Nephrite (Healing)
- Jade, white Jadeite (Healing)
- Jasper, Brecciated **(Foundation)**
- Jasper, Bumblebee (Self)
- Jasper, Kambaba **(Foundation)**
- Jasper, Ocean **(Vision)**
- Jasper, red **(Root)**
- Jet (Healing)
- Kunzite **(Heart)**
- Kyanite, black (Channel)
- Kyanite, blue **(Voice)**
- Labradorite **(Vision)**
- Lapis **(Voice)**
- Larimar (Healing)
- Larvikite (Channel)

- Lavender Chalcedony (Healing)
- Lazurite **(Voice)**
- Lepidolite **(Heart)**
- Jet (Healing)
- Kunzite, pink Spodumene **(Heart)**
- Lepidolite, diamond (Source)
- Lepidolite, purple **(Heart)**
- Libyan Gold Tektite (Source)
- Lingam Stone (Healing)
- Malachite **(Heart)**
- Merlinite (Source)
- Meteorite, iron **(Root)**
- Moldavite (Source)
- Moonstone, black (Channel)
- Moonstone, peach (Belly)
- Moonstone, white or rainbow **(Vision)**
- Morion Smoky Quartz (Channel)
- Natrolite **(Vision)**
- Nebulite, Chrome Chalcedony (Source)
- New Jade Serpentine **(Heart)**
- Nuumite **(Channel)**
- Obsidian, Apache Tear (Healing)
- Obsidian, black (Channel)
- Obsidian, Mahogany **(Root)**
- Obsidian, Midnight Lace (Healing)
- Obsidian, Rainbow **(Vision)**
- Obsidian, silver and golden (Channel)
- Onyx, black (Healing)
- Opal, colorful **(Vision)**
- Opal, green (Belly)

- Opal, light or white **(Root)**
- Opal, pink (Healing)
- Opal, Satin Flash **(Root)**
- Orpiment (Channel)
- Peridot (Source)
- Petalite (Healing)
- Phenacite (Source)
- Pink Halite (Healing)
- Pinolith **(Foundation)**
- Prehnite, blue **(Voice)**
- Prehnite, green (Healing)
- Psilomelane (Self)
- Pyrite (Self)
- Pyrite Concretion (Source)
- Rhodochrosite **(Root)**
- Rhodonite **(Root)**
- Rhyolite **(Vision)**
- Richterite **(Vision)**
- Ruby **(Root)**
- Sapphire, blue **(Vision)**
- Scheelite, golden (Self)
- Scolecite (Healing)
- Selenite, Mexican (Healing)
- Selenite, Moroccan (Channel)
- Seraphinite **(Vision)**
- Serpentine (Heart)
- Shattuckite **(Vision)**
- Shungite (Channel)

- Sodalite **(Vision)**
- Spinel, octahedral (Source)
- Stibnite, gray metallic crystals **(Root)**
- Stilbite, peach (Healing)
- Spodumene, pink Kunzite **(Heart)**
- Spodumene, green Hiddenite (Source)
- Spodumene, Triphane (Source)
- Stromatolite **(Foundation)**
- Sugilite **(Voice)**
- Sunstone (Self)
- Tanzanite **(Vision)**
- Tektite, black (Channel)
- Tiger Eye, blue/black (Self)
- Tiger Eye, red (Self)
- Tiger Eye, yellow (Self)
- Tiger Iron **(Root)**
- Topaz, clear **(Voice)**
- Tourmaline, black (Channel)
- Tourmaline, blue (Source)
- Tourmaline, green (Source)
- Tourmaline, pink **(Heart)**
- Tourmaline, Watermelon **(Heart)**
- Turquoise **(Voice)**
- Ulexite **(Vision)**
- Unakite **(Heart)**
- Ventifact (Channel)
- Zincite (Source)
- Zoisite **(Heart)**

Conclusion

Preparing this book has been transformative. Over the span of six months, I've put 33 years of experience into just a couple hundred pages. My 177 images capture a cross section of notable pieces from my collection, and tell a visual story that adds so much dimension to my words.

I'd like for this book to be a resource for you to return to. I hope it helps you to make sense of the Crystal World—not just with reference to understanding particular stones conceptually, but also regarding how to work with them and apply them in your life. The goal, after all, is to use stones to enhance your clarity and flow. In doing so, we are best able to ride the waves of this life with adaptability and a sense of fulfillment.

If there were three take-home messages I'd like to leave you with, they'd be: embrace both inspiration and logic, come to terms with both the seen and the unseen, and know that every rule has its exceptions.

You can always reach out to me for clarifications, new revelations, and deeper understandings.

My website is **CrystalConcentrics.com** and I'd welcome hearing from you!

SOURCE   IMAGE 177

JEWELRY PENDANT of MOLDAVITE (Chlum locality, Czech Republic), more on page 79 + 177

Message-bringer from On-High

Acknowledgements

First thanks to you, who've read this entire book, and whose life will hopefully be enriched by having experienced it.

I appreciate each and every one of my clients, customers, and friends who really get crystals—what it is that I do with them—and have helped me over the years to help them.

I am grateful to my professional team, everyone who's worked with me technically to make this book a reality.

To my wife Nina, who has supported me ceaselessly in the pursuit of my dreams, and to my children—Kobi and Ruby—who have each put their shoulders to the wheel in moving us forward together.

To generosity and paying it forward. That impulse of Robert Simmons back in 1987—to hand me a Moldavite—it transformed my life.

And last but not least, to my actual and heavenly parents—G8D, guides and guardians—for having carried me through difficult times and lifted me up when I have fallen. May my efforts ever strive to fulfill Your will and good wishes.

Index